Level
2

P9-DUS-090

First Steps in Academic Writing

SECOND EDITION

Ann Hogue

PEARSON
Longman

First Steps in Academic Writing, Second Edition

Pearson Education, 10 Bank Street, White Plains, NY 10606

Staff credits: The people who made up the *First Steps in Academic Writing* team, representing editorial,
production, design, and manufacturing, are: Rhea Banker, Wendy Campbell, Elizabeth
Carlson, Gina DiLillo, Christine Edmonds, Laura Le Dréan, Linda Moser, Edith Pullman, and
Kathleen Silloway.
Cover design: Jill Lehan
Cover images: Egyptian hieroglyphics, close-up by Neil Beer. Getty Images.
Text composition: Integra
Text font: 12/13.5 Times
Illustrator credits: Steve Attoe (pp. 60, 65, 91, 137); Suzanne Mogensen (pp. 73, 85, 98, 106); Jill Wood (pp. 3, 38, 44, 48, 95, 96, 97)
Text credits: p. 166, "Kilt-wearing teen seeks dress code change: Principal sparks debate after telling student to wear pants at school
dance." Used with permission of The Associated Press Copyright 2006. All rights reserved.
Photo credits: p. 1 Doug Menuez/Getty Images; **p. 18** © David Turnley/Corbis; **p. 24** © Bettmann/Corbis; **p. 33** Arthur Tilley/Getty
Images; **p. 55** © Burke/Triolo Productions/Brand X/Corbis; **p. 68** ©Visions of America, LLC/Alamy; **p. 94** © Visions of America,
LLC/Alamy; **p. 102** JG Photography/Alamy; **p.121** Jack Hollingsworth/Getty Images; **p. 124** © Andy Rouse/Corbis; **p. 126** ©
Marvin Koner/Corbis; **p. 128** (top) Transtock Inc./Alamy, (bottom) Motoring Picture Library/Alamy; **p. 145** Mark Boulton/Alamy;
p. 147 AP Images; **p. 156** Ian Shaw/Alamy; **p. 166** M Stock/Alamy

Library of Congress Cataloging-in-Publication Data
Hogue, Ann.
    First steps in academic writing / Ann Hogue. — 2nd ed.
        p.   cm.
    Includes bibliographical references and index.
    ISBN 0-13-241488-0 (student book : alk. paper) — ISBN 0-13-241490-2 (answer key : alk. paper)
    1. English language—Rhetoric.   2. Academic writing.   I. Title.
    PE1478.H57 2007
    808'.042—dc22

                                                                                                    2007022180

LONGMAN ON THE **WEB**

Pearsonlongman.com offers online
resources for teachers and students. Access
our Companion Websites, our online catalog,
and our local offices around the world.

Visit us at **Pearsonlongman.com**.

Printed in the United States of America
8 9 10 —V004—13 12 11 10

Contents

APPENDICES

Preface

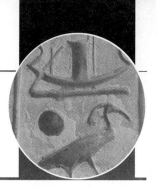

First Steps in Academic Writing, Second Edition, is a high-beginning writing textbook/workbook for English language learners in academic settings. It teaches rhetoric and sentence structure in a straightforward manner, using a step-by-step approach, high-interest models, and varied practices.

Students are guided through the writing process to produce well-organized, clearly developed paragraphs. Simple explanations are supported by clear examples to help students through typical rough spots, and numerous practices help students assimilate each skill.

The book contains six chapters. Chapter 1 introduces the concept and form of the paragraph, and Chapter 2 teaches paragraph structure. Chapters 2–6 focus on writing instructions, descriptions, and expressing opinions; they teach students several standard patterns of organization as well. Each chapter also provides instruction in punctuation and in sentence structure, starting with simple sentences and progressing through compound and complex sentences. Each chapter also guides students step-by-step through the writing process as they work on their writing assignments.

What's New in the Second Edition

Instructors familiar with the First Edition will find a few changes, made in response to the comments of reviewers and teachers who have used the First Edition over the years.

- Paragraph structure is presented earlier, in Chapter 2.
- Work on topic sentences has been greatly expanded to include many more examples and practices.
- A section on the ordering of adjectives has been added to assist students in writing vivid descriptions.
- Some models and practice items have been updated or replaced. Old favorites have been retained.
- Mid-chapter writing assignments are now Try It Out! practices, allowing students to try out new skills without the pressure of being graded on their efforts.
- Journal writing has been added as an option.
- There are separate worksheets for self-editing (Writer's Self-Check) and peer editing (Reader's Response).
- Business letter writing has become an optional, change-of-pace lesson in Appendix F at the back of the book.

Organization of the Chapters

Each chapter has the following three sections: Organization, Sentence Structure, and Writing. Most chapters have a fourth section containing lessons on grammar, punctuation, and/or rules for capitalization.

Chapter Preview

Each chapter begins with a list of the learning goals for the chapter and a prewriting activity that prepares the student to write a paragraph a few pages later.

Organization Sections

In the Organization sections in Chapters 1 and 2, students learn paragraph format and paragraph structure. In Chapters 2–4, they learn to organize their paragraphs using listing order, time order, and spatial order (description). In Chapter 5, they learn to develop their paragraphs using reasons and examples, and in Chapter 6, they focus on expressing an opinion with adequate support.

An overview of the writing process appears in Chapter 1, using a recurring model on a topic similar to the Writing Assignment for that chapter. Students learn various prewriting techniques, starting with freewriting in Chapter 1 and proceeding to listing, clustering, and outlining in subsequent chapters.

Sentence Structure Sections

A good portion of each chapter provides students with opportunities to improve the structure of their sentences. Simple sentences are the focus in Chapter 1, compound sentences in Chapter 2, and complex sentences in Chapters 3, 5, and 6. Chapter 4 teaches students to vary their sentence structure by moving prepositional phrases.

Writing Sections

Each Writing section reviews the points covered in the chapter prior to the Writing Assignment. The Writing Assignment for each chapter contains clear step-by-step instructions. Students are never left wondering how to begin or what to do next. Because students will have encountered the topic for the Writing Assignment earlier in the chapter, they will have thought about or discussed the topic before they tackle writing about it.

Models

Students see several writing models in each chapter. Each Organization section contains a model paragraph that demonstrates the rhetorical forms taught in that chapter. Some Sentence Structure sections also begin with a model that demonstrates both the rhetorical mode just taught and the sentence structures just ahead. In addition, many practice exercises serve double duty—as models and as exercises.

Questions on the Models

Following each model are Questions on the Model that focus the students' attention on specific elements in the paragraph. These questions either help students consolidate material taught in previous chapters or prepare them for the learning task ahead. For example, questions may ask students to locate the topic sentence, identify the steps in a how-to paragraph, find prepositional phrases, or notice facts that support reasons in an opinion paragraph.

In-Class Writing

Group prewriting and in-class writing of the first drafts are especially helpful for beginning students because the instructor is available for immediate consultation. Also, the instructor can check to make sure everyone is on the right track. Pair and group collaboration is appropriate for prewriting and editing work; however, writing is essentially an individual task even when done in class.

Explanations and Examples

Beginning students grasp points more easily by seeing several examples rather than by reading long explanations. Therefore, explanations are brief, and examples are numerous. Important information, such as commas rules, charts of transition signals, and sentence "formulas," is boxed.

Practice Exercises

Each teaching point is accompanied by a variety of practice exercises, which progress from recognition exercises to controlled production to communicative Try It Out! practices.

Appendices

There are seven appendices at the back of the book for students' easy reference. Teachers might point them out to students early in the term.

Appendix A   Journal Writing
Appendix B   Correction Symbols
Appendix C   Grammar Words and Kinds of Sentences
Appendix D   Conjunctions
Appendix E   Transition Signals
Appendix F   Business Letters
Appendix G   Reader's Response and Writer's Self-Check Worksheets

Journal Writing   Chapter 1 introduces students to journal writing and shows them how to do it. Appendix A contains topic suggestions. Teachers are urged to introduce journal writing early in the term, for journal writing is particularly valuable for students at the beginning level to develop writing fluency.

Editing Worksheets   Appendix G contains peer-editing (Reader's Response) and self-editing (Writer's Self-Check) worksheets for each mid-chapter Try It Out! and each end-of-chapter Writing Assignment. Instructors can use one or the other, or both, as they prefer. Peer editors can write their comments on the worksheet. Alternatively, each student can read his or her draft aloud in a small group of classmates and then elicit oral comments and suggestions by asking the checklist questions. The student who has read then records the group's suggestions on his or her own paper. Instructors can also respond to student writing by using the peer-editing checklist.

Answer Key

An Answer Key is available upon request from the publisher.

Acknowledgments

I sincerely appreciate the contributions of the many people who have helped shape this second edition of *First Steps in Academic Writing*. First and foremost, I thank Executive Editor Laura Le Dréan for her unflagging patience, support, and guidance. I also thank her assistant Wendy Campbell for photo research, and Caroline Gibbs of City College of San Francisco for permission to use her excellent material on Journal Writing.

To the many users of the first edition who took the time to offer suggestions, I extend my heartfelt thanks: **Sandy Abouda**, Seminole Community College, Florida; **Vicki Blaho**, Santa Monica College, California; **Barbara Bonander**, College of Marin, California; **Jeff Cady**, College of Marin, California; **Jackye Cumby**, Mercer University, Georgia; **Diana Davidson del Toro**, Cuyamaca College, California; **Greg Davis**, Portland State University, Oregon; **Diane Harris**, Imperial Valley College, California; **Mohammed Iqbal**, City College of San Francisco, California; **Linda Lieberman**, College of Marin, California; **Mark Neville**, ALHOSN University, United Arab Emirates; **Kim Sano**, Aoyama Gakuin Women's Junior College, Tokyo; **Laura Shier**, Portland State University, Oregon; **Christine Tierney**, Houston Community College, Texas. I hope you recognize the many places where your comments and advice improved the book.

Introducing People

What Is Academic Writing?

The kind of writing you will do in this class is called **academic writing** because it is the kind of writing you do in college classes. Every kind of writing has a particular purpose and a particular audience. The purpose of academic writing is to explain something or to give information about something. Its audience is your teacher and your classmates.

Academic writing requires certain skills. These skills include **sentence structure** (how to arrange words in a sentence), **organization** (how to arrange ideas in a paragraph), and, of course, **grammar** and **punctuation**. Each chapter of this book has sections with a lesson and practices for each skill. At the end of each chapter, you will write a paragraph using the skills you have just learned.

Chapter Preview

In Chapter 1, you will write paragraphs about people. Your first paragraph will be about a classmate. You will also study and practice:

- paragraph form
- subjects, verbs, and objects
- simple sentences
- six rules for capitalization
- four steps in the writing process
- journal writing

Your last paragraph at the end of the chapter will be about a person who has made a difference in your life, in your community, or in the world.

Prewriting Activity: Asking Questions and Taking Notes

Whenever you write, you need ideas to write about. Taking notes is one way to get ideas. In this activity, you will ask a classmate some questions and take notes about his or her answers. When you take notes, you do not have to write complete sentences. Just write down the important information.

1. Look at the topics in the following chart. With your class, make up questions about the topics to ask a classmate. Your teacher will write the questions on the chalkboard.

   Note: There are some personal questions that are not OK to ask. Discuss with the class which questions are OK to ask and which ones you should not ask.

Sample Questions | **Sample Notes of Classmate Responses**

What is your first name? — Santy

What is your family name? — Valverde

Where are you from? — Michoacan, Mexico

How long have you lived
in this country? — 2 years

2. Choose a partner and ask him or her the questions. Take notes by writing the answers in the chart. Keep the chart. You will use it later to write a paragraph about your classmate.

3. Introduce your classmate by telling his or her answers to the class or to a small group.

OK to Ask	Not OK to Ask	Topics	Classmate's Answers (Notes)
☑	☐	First name and family name	_____
☐	☒	Age	_____
☐	☐	City and country	_____
☐	☐	Family status	_____
☐	☐	Religion	_____
☐	☐	Address in this country	_____
☐	☐	Length of time in this country	_____
☐	☐	Length of time studying English	_____
☐	☐	Reasons for studying English	_____
☐	☐	Job or occupation	_____
☐	☐	Salary	_____
☐	☐	Hobbies or sports	_____
☐	☐	Weekend activities	_____
☐	☐	Plans for the future	_____

(*You and your classmates may add other questions.*)

_____   _____

_____   _____

PART 1 | Organization

What Is a Paragraph?

A **paragraph** is a group of related sentences about a single topic. The topic of a paragraph is one, and only one, idea.

A paragraph has three main parts.

1. **Topic sentence**
   The first sentence in a paragraph is a sentence that names the topic and tells what the paragraph will explain about the topic. This sentence is called the **topic sentence**.

2. **Supporting sentences**
   The middle sentences in a paragraph are called the **supporting sentences**. Supporting sentences give examples or other details about the topic.

3. **Concluding sentence**
   The last sentence in a paragraph is called the **concluding sentence**. A concluding sentence often repeats the topic sentence in different words or summarizes the main points.

A paragraph is like a cheeseburger sandwich: two pieces of bread (the topic and concluding sentences) enclosing the filling (the supporting sentences).

Topic Sentence

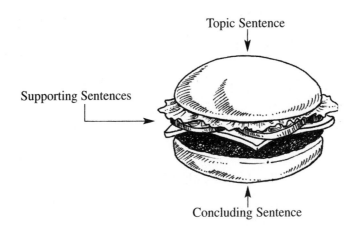

Supporting Sentences

Concluding Sentence

Each paragraph that you write for this class should also have a **title**. A title tells the topic of the paragraph in a few words. A title is short. It is not a complete sentence. It may be just one word. Here are some examples of titles.

My Classmate

Friendship

A Famous Soccer Player

As you read the following model, look for the three parts of a paragraph.

MODEL

What Is a Paragraph?

Paragraph 1

Mrs. Robinson

¹My first grade teacher was an important person in my life. ²Her name was Mrs. Robinson. ³In the schools in my country, children usually learn to print before they learn to write. ⁴Mrs. Robinson didn't believe in printing. ⁵She thought it was a waste of time. ⁶She taught us to write in cursive script (like handwriting) from the first day. ⁷At first it was hard. ⁸She made us practice a lot. ⁹I remember filling entire pages just with capital *O*s. ¹⁰At the end of the year, we felt very grown up because we could write in cursive. ¹¹Mrs. Robinson was important in my life because she taught me a valuable lesson. ¹²I can achieve anything by working hard.

Paragraph 2

My Best Friend

¹My best friend, Freddie, has three important qualities. ²First of all, Freddie is always ready to have fun. ³Sometimes we play Frisbee in the park. ⁴Sometimes we just sit around in my room, listening to music and talking. ⁵Well, I talk. ⁶Freddie just listens. ⁷Second, he is completely trustworthy. ⁸I can tell Freddie my deepest secrets, and he doesn't share them with anyone else. ⁹Third, Freddie understands my moods. ¹⁰When I am angry, he tries to make me feel better. ¹¹When I am sad, he tries to comfort me. ¹²When I am happy, he is happy too. ¹³To sum up, my best friend is fun to be with, trustworthy, and understanding—even if he is just a dog.

You will study the three parts of a paragraph in more detail in Chapter 2. For now, just remember that a paragraph has three parts.

Paragraph Form

In academic writing, there is a special form for paragraphs. When you write a paragraph, make it look like the one below.

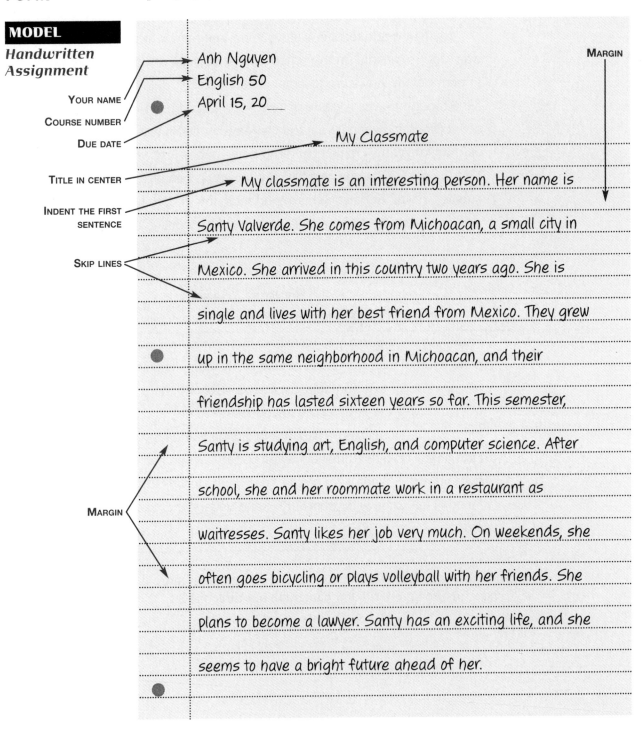

MODEL

Handwritten Assignment

YOUR NAME
COURSE NUMBER
DUE DATE

TITLE IN CENTER

INDENT THE FIRST SENTENCE

SKIP LINES

MARGIN

MARGIN

Anh Nguyen
English 50
April 15, 20___

My Classmate

My classmate is an interesting person. Her name is

Santy Valverde. She comes from Michoacan, a small city in

Mexico. She arrived in this country two years ago. She is

single and lives with her best friend from Mexico. They grew

up in the same neighborhood in Michoacan, and their

friendship has lasted sixteen years so far. This semester,

Santy is studying art, English, and computer science. After

school, she and her roommate work in a restaurant as

waitresses. Santy likes her job very much. On weekends, she

often goes bicycling or plays volleyball with her friends. She

plans to become a lawyer. Santy has an exciting life, and she

seems to have a bright future ahead of her.

Here are the rules for correct paragraph form for handwritten paragraphs:

1. **Paper**
   Use 8½-inch-by-11-inch lined, 3-hole paper. The three holes should be on your left side as you write. Write on one side of the paper only.

2. **Ink**

Use black or dark blue ink only.

3. **Heading**

Write your full name in the upper left corner. On the next line, write the course name and number. On the third line, write the date the assignment is due in the order month-day-year, with a comma after the day.

4. **Assignment Title**

Center the title of your paragraph on the first line.

5. **Body**

Skip one line, and start your writing on the third line. Indent (move to the right) the first sentence ½ inch from the left margin.

6. **Margins**

Leave a 1-inch margin on the left and right sides of the paper. Also leave a 1-inch margin at the bottom of the page. Your teacher uses these empty spaces to write comments to you.

7. **Spacing**

Leave a blank line between each line of writing. Your teacher uses the space between lines to mark corrections.

If you use a computer, make your paper look like this:

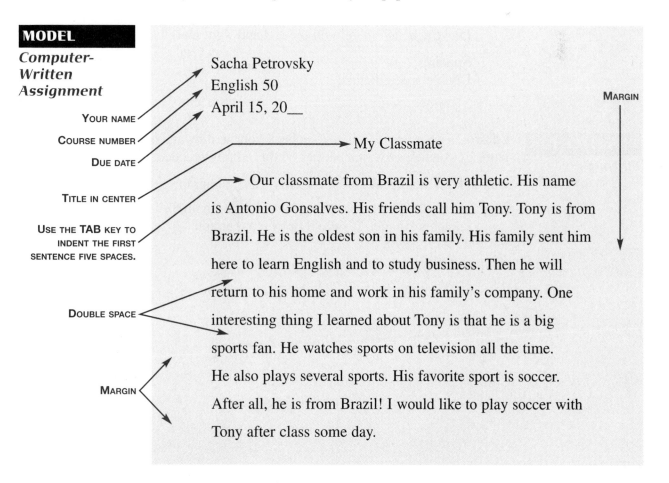

MODEL

Computer-Written Assignment

YOUR NAME

COURSE NUMBER

DUE DATE

TITLE IN CENTER

USE THE **TAB** KEY TO INDENT THE FIRST SENTENCE FIVE SPACES.

DOUBLE SPACE

MARGIN

MARGIN

Sacha Petrovsky

English 50

April 15, 20___

My Classmate

Our classmate from Brazil is very athletic. His name is Antonio Gonsalves. His friends call him Tony. Tony is from Brazil. He is the oldest son in his family. His family sent him here to learn English and to study business. Then he will return to his home and work in his family's company. One interesting thing I learned about Tony is that he is a big sports fan. He watches sports on television all the time. He also plays several sports. His favorite sport is soccer. After all, he is from Brazil! I would like to play soccer with Tony after class some day.

Here are the rules for correct paragraph form for a paragraph typed on a computer.

1. **Paper**
   Use 8½-inch-by-11-inch white paper.

2. **Font**
   Use a standard font style, such as Times New Roman. Do not use underlining, italics, or bold type to emphasize words. It is not correct to do so in academic writing.

3. **Heading**
   Type your full name in the upper left corner. On the next line, type the course number. On the third line of the heading, type the date the assignment is due in the order month-day-year, with a comma after the day.

4. **Assignment Title**
   Skip one line, and then center your title. Use the centering icon on your word processing program.

5. **Body**
   Skip one line, and start typing on the third line. Indent (move to the right) the first line of each paragraph by using the TAB key. (The TAB key automatically indents five spaces.)

6. **Margins**
   Leave a 1-inch margin on the left and right margins.

7. **Spacing**
   Double-space the body.

PRACTICE 1

Editing Paragraph Form

Editing is what you do when you check your writing and correct and improve it. Work by yourself or with a partner on this editing practice.

Step 1 Find the mistakes in the form of this paragraph.

Step 2 Copy the paragraph using correct form on an 8½-by-11-inch piece of notebook paper. It should be *one* paragraph.

Writing class   Amy Wong

Monday

My Classmate

My classmate is a very nice person. Her name is Phuong Pham. She is from Vietnam. In Vietnam she was a pharmacist.

She is married.

She lives with her husband, her children, and her parents-in-law in a house. Phuong is taking an art class, two English classes, computer science, and math.

She likes to listen to music and to read books.

She doesn't have a job right now but plans to get one when she finishes school.

Try It Out! Write a paragraph about the classmate you interviewed in the Prewriting Activity at the beginning of the chapter.

Step 1 Give your paragraph a title, such as "My Classmate" or "My New Classmate."

Step 2 Begin your paragraph with a topic sentence that tells your classmate's name and also describes his or her personality in general. You may choose a word from the following list to describe your classmate's personality, or you may use a different word. Discuss the meaning of new words with your class.

interesting	talented	cheerful	soft-spoken
friendly	serious	quiet	fun-loving
likeable	energetic	outgoing	hard-working

Here are some examples of topic sentences.

My new classmate is an interesting young woman.

My classmate is an energetic young man.

My new classmate is a friendly person.

Writer's Tip

Do NOT tell a specific fact about your classmate in your first sentence. For example, do not begin your paragraph with a sentence such as *My classmate is from China* or *My classmate is married*.

Step 3 Write several sentences telling about your classmate. Use your notes from the chart on page 3 to make sentences.

Step 4 End your paragraph with a concluding sentence that tells how you feel about your classmate.

I am happy to have Alex as my classmate.

I think Amy and I will become good friends.

I would like to play soccer with Tony after class some day.

Step 5 Check your paragraph.

- First, read your paragraph to the classmate whom you wrote about. Then ask him or her to complete Reader's Response 1A on page 190. Then decide together if you should make changes in your paragraph.

- Second, check your paragraph against Writer's Self-Check 1A on page 191.

Step 6 Write a neat final copy of your paragraph to hand in to your teacher. Your teacher may also ask you to hand in your prewriting and your other drafts.

PART 2 | Grammar and Capitalization

What Is a Sentence?

In the Organization section of this chapter, you learned that a paragraph is a group of sentences about one topic. How do you know what a sentence is? Here is a definition.

> A **sentence** is a group of words that contains a subject and a verb and expresses a complete thought. A sentence begins with a capital letter and ends with a period.[1]

---

[1] A sentence may also end with a question mark or exclamation point, but in academic writing, most sentences end with a period.

These are sentences:

1. He is a student.
2. It is hot today.
3. He looks tired.
4. Are you hungry?
5. Who's there?
6. Hurry!
7. The man bought a new car.
8. Does your sister live with you?
9. Where did you buy that hat?
10. Don't be late.

These are not sentences:

11. Is very athletic. (*There is no subject.*)

    In some languages, you can leave out a pronoun subject (*he, she, it, we, you,* and *they*) when the meaning is clear without it. English requires a subject in every sentence. (*Exception*: See Command Sentences on page 12.)

    CORRECTED: **He** is very athletic.

12. The baby sleepy. (*There is no verb.*)

    In some languages, you can leave out a verb like *is* or *are* when the meaning is clear without it. English requires a verb in every sentence.

    CORRECTED: The baby **is** sleepy.

13. The man bought. (*This is not a complete thought. What did the man buy?*)

    Many verbs in English require an object. (An object is a noun or pronoun that follows a verb.) Some of these verbs are *buy, give, have, like, love, need, own, place, put, spend,* and *want.*

    OBJECT
    CORRECTED: The man bought **a cup of coffee**.

14. When I finish my education. (*This is not a complete thought. What will happen when I finish my education?*)

    A group of words that begins with *when, if,* or *because* (and others) is only half of a sentence. You must join it to another subject and verb to make a complete thought.

    CORRECTED: When I finish my education, I will work for my uncle.

You will learn more about these half-sentences in Chapter 3.

Command Sentences

If a sentence gives a command or instruction, we understand that the subject is *you*, but we don't say or write *you*. The verb in a command sentence is always in the simple (dictionary) form—*stop, go, wait, be, eat*. To make a command negative, put *don't* in front of the verb.

Commands	Negative Commands
(~~You~~) Be quiet.	(~~You~~) Don't eat so much!
(~~You~~) Wait for me!	(~~You~~) Don't forget to call home.
(~~You~~) Speak slowly.	(~~You~~) Don't worry.

PRACTICE 2

Recognizing Sentences

A. Which two sentences in examples 1–10 on page 11 are commands? Underline their verbs.

B. Work with a partner.

Step 1 Read each group of words out loud.

Step 2 Decide which ones are complete sentences and which ones are not.

Step 3 Write *S* (for sentence) next to complete sentences and *NS* (for not a sentence) next to word groups that are not sentences.

Step 4 Explain why the *NS* word groups are not sentences.

1. _NS_   Is very hot today. (__There is no subject.__)

2. _S_   It is very hot today. (_____)

3. ____   My new classmate from Brazil. (_____)

4. ____   He speaks three languages fluently. (_____)

5. ____   Is very handsome. (_____)

6. ____   He wants to start his own business. (_____)

7. ____   He isn't married. (_____)

8. ____   Enjoys many sports, especially baseball. (_____)

9. ____   Don't sleep in class. (_____)

10. ____   The children hungry. (_____)

11. ____   They didn't like. (_____)

12. ____   They don't want. (_____)

13. ____   Go to bed! (_____)

Subjects, Verbs, and Objects

In English, the subject of a sentence is *always* expressed (except in commands).

> The **subject** tells who or what did something. It is a noun or pronoun.

My roommate lost his keys.
(Who lost his keys?—my roommate)

The taxi hit the child.
(What hit the child?—the taxi)

Soccer and tennis are my favorite sports.
(What are my favorite sports?—soccer and tennis)

> The **verb** usually tells an action. Sometimes a verb doesn't tell an action. Sometimes it just links the subject with the rest of the sentence.

Action verbs name an action, such as *hit, live, lose, speak, go*, and *come*.

The taxi **hit** the child.

My family **lives** in a two-bedroom apartment.

My roommate **lost** his keys.

Linking verbs link the subject with the rest of the sentence. Linking verbs do not have objects. The most common linking verbs are *be, become, look, feel, seem, smell, sound*, and *taste*.

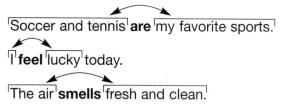

Soccer and tennis **are** my favorite sports.
I **feel** lucky today.
The air **smells** fresh and clean.

> The **object** receives the action of an action verb. It is a noun or pronoun.

To find an object, make a question by putting *what* after an action verb. (*Note*: This method for finding objects doesn't work with linking verbs because linking verbs do not have objects.)

The taxi hit **the child**.
(Hit what?—the child. The child is an object.)

My roommate lost **his keys**.
(Lost what?—his keys. His keys is an object.)

His girlfriend found **them**.
(Found what?—them. Them is an object.)

Not all sentences have objects.

My family lives in a two-bedroom apartment.
(Lives what?—not possible. This sentence has no object.)

The sun is shining today.
(Is shining what?—not possible. This sentence has no object.)

The fish didn't smell fresh.
(Didn't smell what?—not possible. This sentence has no object.)

Writer's Tip

Certain verbs MUST have objects. Some of these verbs are *buy, give, have, like, love, need, own, place, put, spend,* and *want*.

They need **some money**.

I don't want **it**.

PRACTICE 3

Subjects, Verbs, and Objects

Identify subjects, verbs, and objects in sentences.

Step 1 Underline the subjects with one line.

Step 2 Underline the verbs with two lines.

Step 3 Circle the objects.

Step 4 Write *S*, *V*, or *O* above each underlined or circled word.

1. My youngest brother is in high school. (There is no object.)

2. He watches TV and does homework at the same time.

3. He works at a shopping mall.

4. He likes his job but doesn't like his boss.

5. His job is easy and pays well.

6. This semester, he is taking extra classes.

7. He will go to college next year.

8. He speaks and understands English very well.

9. On weekends, he and his friends play soccer.

10. He doesn't have a girlfriend yet.

Step 1 Look for missing subjects and verbs.

Step 2 Add the missing words. (There may be more than one possible answer.)

Larry's Bad Habit

                                    is
¹My friend Larry has a bad habit. ²He ︿ never on time to anything. ³Arrives ten minutes late everywhere. ⁴Larry always an excuse. ⁵"I missed the bus." ⁶"My alarm clock didn't ring." ⁷"My watch stopped." ⁸"My mother telephoned me just as I was leaving." ⁹He uses each excuse at least twice a week. ¹⁰I know them all. ¹¹Whenever Larry rushes in—ten minutes late, of course—and starts to say, "Sorry I'm late, but I . . ." or "Sorry I'm late, but my . . ." or "Sorry I'm late, but my mother . . .," I can finish the sentence for him. ¹²Larry's bad habit not a problem for me any longer. ¹³If the movie at 7:00, I tell Larry it starts at 6:45. ¹⁴Then he early!

Step 1 Decide where sentences begin and end. (There are 14 sentences.)

Step 2 Add a period at the end of each sentence, and change the first letter of each new sentence to a capital.

My Neighbors

a young couple from India lives next door to me the husband's name is Ajay the wife's name is Anjuli everyone calls her Anju they have a young son and are expecting their second child in a few weeks they hope to have a girl this time both Ajay and Anju have good jobs he is an executive in a computer company she is a computer programmer and works in our local hospital Anju is a wonderful cook she cooks mostly Indian food they sometimes invite neighbors on weekends for a potluck meal¹ we all bring something to share it is fun to live next door to Ajay and Anju.

---

¹potluck meal: meal to which everyone contributes a dish to share

Capitalization: Six Rules   In English, there are many rules for using capital letters. Here are six important ones.

Rules	Examples	
Capitalize:		
1. The first word in a sentence.	**M**y neighbor is a mechanic.	
2. The pronoun *I*.	My friends and **I** often study together.	
3. Names of people and their titles.	King **A**bdullah II	
	President **P**utin	
	Professor **I**ndiana **J**ones	
	Mr. and **M**rs. **H**omer **S**impson	
BUT NOT a title without a name.	He's a king.	
	Have you met your math professor?	
Exception: A title without a name is sometimes capitalized if it refers to a specific person.	The **P**resident of the **U**nited **S**tates had dinner with the **E**mperor of **J**apan.	
4. Nationalities, languages, religions, and ethnic groups.	**S**wedish	**J**ewish
	English	**C**hristian
	Spanish	**A**sian
	Farsi	**H**ispanic
	Muslim	**N**ative **A**merican
5. Names of school courses with numbers.	**P**sychology 101	
Note: Don't capitalize school subjects except names of nationalities, languages, religions, and college classes with numbers.	history	**R**ussian history
	math	**H**istory 101
	physics	**P**hysics 352
6. Specific places you could find on a map.	Lake **T**iticaca	**E**ngland
	the **N**orth **P**ole	**F**irst **S**treet
	South **A**merica	**T**imes **S**quare
	Amazon **R**iver	**N**ew **Y**ork **C**ity

PRACTICE 6

Capitalization

Write your own examples for capitalization rules 3–6. Ask your teacher for help with spelling, or use a dictionary.

Rule 3

a queen _Queen Noor_____

a president _____

a doctor _____

a mayor or governor _____

Rule 4

a language _____

a nationality _____

a religion _____

Rule 5

a school subject without a number _____

a college class with a number _____

Rule 6

a street _____

a city or town _____

a state _____

a country _____

a sea or an ocean _____

an island _____

a lake _____

a river _____

a park _____

a square _____

PRACTICE 7

Editing for Capitalization

Nelson Mandela

Change the small letters to capital letters wherever necessary in the following paragraph.

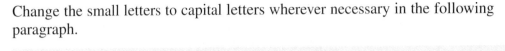

N   M
~~n~~elson ~~m~~andela

[1]my name is nelson mandela, and i have had an unusual life. [2]i have been both a prisoner and a president in my country. [3]i was born in 1918 in a small village in south africa. [4]my father, henry mandela, was the chief of our tribe.[1] [5]as a child, i took care of the family's cattle and goats. [6]when i grew up, i decided to become a lawyer. [7]this seemed to be a good way to help my people. [8]after i became a lawyer, i became the leader of a group of young africans who wanted to change the system of discrimination[2] in our country. [9]because of my political activities, i went to prison for twenty-seven years. [10]the prison was on a cold, windy island in the atlantic ocean. [11]however, the world didn't forget about me. [12]i received important visitors, awards, and university degrees from all over the world. [13]i also learned afrikaans, which is the language of white south africans. [14]of course, i also speak english and xhosa, which is the language of my tribe. [15]in 1990, i was set free. [16]i became the president of south africa in 1994. [17]during my time in office, i tried to bring peace, democracy, and prosperity to all of my country's people. [18]now i am retired.

Journal Writing

A journal is a notebook in which you write about your life and your thoughts. Each time you write in your journal, you make a **journal entry**.

Your teacher will not grade your journal, so journal writing is a good way to practice new skills without worrying about a grade. Your teacher will read each entry and make comments. He or she may ask questions for you to answer in your next entry. You can also write questions to your teacher in your journal. A journal can be like a conversation.

---

[1]**tribe:** group of people who live in the same area and have the same customs, beliefs, and leader
[2]**discrimination:** treating one group of people differently from another in an unfair way

Your teacher may ask you to write for a certain amount of time every day or every week, or he or she may ask you to write a certain number of pages. It is a good idea to write the date and your starting and stopping times above each entry. Here is a sample page from a student's journal.

MODEL

Journal Entry

September 13, 20__
Start: 8:15 P.M.
Stop: 8:35 P.M.

Hello! My name is Hamoud al-Rashid. I am from Algeria.

I was born on January 31, 1991. I lived with my parents and

six brothers and sisters in the beautiful city of Oran. Oran is

on the Mediterranean Sea. I attended elementary school

there. When I was fourteen years old, my family moved to

Algiers. I attended Mohamed Ben Othmane High School

there. Then I . . .

Journal Assignment

Your first journal assignment is to introduce yourself to your teacher. Practice what you have learned about capital letters. Include as many proper nouns as possible in order to practice the capitalization rules.

Write about your childhood, your hometown, your family, your education, your hobbies, or anything else that your teacher might find interesting. Leave lots of space for your teacher to make comments or to ask for more information.

For other topics to write about in your journal, see the topic suggestions in Appendix A at the back of the book.

PART 3 | Sentence Structure

Now let's begin to study the different kinds of sentences in English.

There are four kinds of sentences in English: (1) simple, (2) compound, (3) complex, and (4) compound-complex. In this chapter, you will learn about simple sentences.

Simple Sentences

> A **simple sentence** is a sentence that has one subject-verb pair.

The word *simple* in "simple sentence" doesn't mean "easy." It means "one subject-verb pair."

The subject in a simple sentence may be compound:[1]

My brother and I are completely different.

The verb in a simple sentence may be compound:

They **laughed and cried** at the same time.

However, each sentence is a simple sentence because it has only one subject-verb pair.

Analyze the simple sentences in the left column and their "formulas" in the right column. There are many variations, but each sentence has only one SV pair.

Simple Sentences	"Formulas"
S V 1. My younger sister speaks English well.	S V
S S V 2. My mother and father speak English well.	S S V
S S V V 3. My mother and father speak and write English well.	S S V V
S V 4. My parents will retire soon.	S V
S V V 5. Then they will move into a smaller apartment or live with my older brother and his family.	S V V

---

[1]**compound:** In grammar, *compound* means "more than one."

The following sentence is not a simple sentence because it has two subject-verb pairs. The formula looks like this: SV SV. You will learn more about this kind of sentence in Chapter 2.

<u>My brother</u> <u>lives</u> in New York, and <u>my sister</u> <u>lives</u> in Paris.

Writer's Tip

When you look for verbs, count only verbs that change tense.

My grandmother **wants** to learn to drive.
(*Count only* wants. *Do not count* to learn *or* to drive *because they do not change tense. Verbs with* to *in front of them are infinitives. Infinitives never change.*)

My sister **will teach** in exchange for cooking lessons.
(*Count* will teach *as one verb, not two.*)

A duck **is swimming** in the hotel swimming pool.
(*Count only the first* is swimming. *The second* swimming *is not a verb; it is a special kind of adjective called a participle.*)

Swimming **is** my favorite way to exercise.
(*Count only* is. *In this sentence,* swimming *is a special kind of noun called a gerund.*)

PRACTICE 8

Simple Sentence Patterns

A. Identify the formula in the following simple sentences.

Step 1 Underline the subjects with one line.

Step 2 Underline the verbs with two lines.

Step 3 Write *S* above each underlined subject and *V* above each underlined verb.

Step 4 Finally, write the formula for each sentence in the numbered spaces.

My Grandfather

¹<u>My grandfather</u> <u>is</u> old in years but young in spirit. ²Every day, he swims a mile and works in his garden. ³He and my grandmother have four children and ten grandchildren. ⁴My grandfather loves parties and invites our entire family to his house for a big dinner on his birthday.

(continued on next page)

⁵All twenty of us eat and tell stories half the night. ⁶He never gets tired and is always the last to go to bed. ⁷On his last birthday, my brothers and I gave him a present. ⁸We put our money together and bought him a video game system. ⁹Now he invites us to his house every weekend to play video games with him. ¹⁰My grandfather will always seem young to me.

1. <u>S V</u>   3. ____   5. ____   7. ____   9. ____

2. ____   4. ____   6. ____   8. ____   10. ____

B. Work first by yourself, and then with a partner.

   Step 1 Write six simple sentences about your family or family members. Use each of these patterns twice: SV, SSV, SVV.

   Step 2 Show your sentences to your partner. Ask your partner to identify the pattern in each sentence.

   <u>S V V</u> 1.   <u>My youngest brother goes to school</u>

   _____   <u>and works part-time.</u>

   ____ 2. _____

   _____

   ____ 3. _____

   _____

   ____ 4. _____

   _____

   ____ 5. _____

   _____

   ____ 6. _____

   _____

   ____ 7. _____

   _____

Connecting Words: *and, or*

Often you need to connect words or groups of words in a sentence. One way to do this is to use a connecting word. Connecting words are called **conjunctions**. There are many conjunctions in English. Two of the most common ones are *and* and *or*. They have different meanings.

> *And* joins two or more similar things in positive sentences.
>
>> I like Chinese **and** Italian food.
>>
>> We have class on Mondays, Wednesdays, **and** Fridays.
>
> *Or* connects two or more similar things in negative sentences.
>
>> I don't like warm milk **or** cold coffee.
>>
>> We don't have class on Tuesdays **or** Thursdays.
>
> *Or* also connects two or more choices or alternatives.
>
>> I would like to go to London, Rome, **or** Paris on my next vacation. (*I cannot go to all three places. I will choose one.*)
>>
>> My father **or** my mother will meet me at the airport. (*This sentence means that only one person will come to the airport. Compare*: My father and my mother will meet me at the airport. *This sentence means that two people will come to the airport.*)

Use this chart to help you remember the meanings of *and* and *or* in a simple sentence.

+	+	Use *and* to join two or more items in a positive sentence. I love tacos, pizza, **and** egg rolls.
–	–	Use *or* to join two or more items in a negative sentence. I don't like hot dogs **or** hamburgers.
T?	F?	Also, use *or* to connect choices. Is this sentence true **or** false? Do you want to stay home **or** go out tonight?

PRACTICE 9

*Using **and, or***

Combine the two sentences in each pair to make one sentence. Use *and* or *or* according to the meaning. Try not to repeat any words.

1. I like chocolate ice cream. I like coffee ice cream.

   <u>I like chocolate and coffee ice cream.</u>

2. I can speak English. I can understand English.

   _____

3. I can't speak Tagalog. I can't speak Vietnamese.

   _____

4. Blue is my favorite color. Yellow is my favorite color. (*Be sure to make the verb and the word* color *plural*.)

   _____

5. Would you like soup? Would you like salad? (*You can have only one.*)

   _____

6. You can eat your pizza here. You can take it home.

   _____

   _____

Helen Keller

7. Helen Keller, a famous American woman, was blind. Helen Keller, a famous American woman, was deaf.

   _____

   _____

8. She could not see. She could not hear.

   _____

9. With the help of her teacher, Helen learned to speak. Helen became a famous spokesperson for handicapped people all over the world.

   _____

   _____

Sentence Combining

Sentence combining is a way to improve your sentence-writing skills. When you do a sentence-combining exercise like the Practice you just completed, you combine two (or more) short sentences into one longer sentence. All the long sentences together make a paragraph.

There may be several correct ways to combine the sentences. However, there are a few rules to follow.

1. Don't repeat words if possible. For example, in example 1 below, don't repeat *I am*.
2. You may omit words, but don't leave out any important information.
3. You may change words. For example, you may change a noun to a pronoun or make a singular word plural.
4. You may add words. For example, in example 2, you need to add the connecting word *and*.

Your goal is to write smooth, grammatically correct sentences that contain all the information but do not repeat any of it.

Example 1

    a. I am a man.

    b. I am famous.

Combined sentence: <u>I am a famous man.</u>

I am a man and I am famous is a grammatically correct sentence, but a native speaker would not write it because a native speaker would not repeat the words *I am*. Another possible sentence is *I am a man who is famous*, but this sentence contains unnecessary words.

Example 2

    a. I have white hair.

    b. I have a long white beard.

Combined sentence: <u>I have white hair and a long white beard.</u>

You must keep the word *white* in the expressions *white hair* and *a long white beard* because it is important information.

Try It Out!   **Step 1** Combine the sentences in each pair to make one sentence. There may be more than one correct way to combine the sentences.

Step 2 Write your new sentences in paragraph form. Do not number the sentences, and do not write them in a list. Write them as a paragraph.

Who Am I?

1. a. I am a cartoon animal.

    b. I am famous.

    I am a famous cartoon animal.

2. a. I have big ears.

    b. I have black ears.

    _____

3. a. I always wear red shorts.

    b. I always wear white gloves.

    _____

4. a. I look like an animal.

    b. I talk like a human.

    _____

5. a. I live in a place called Disneyland.

    b. I work in a place called Disneyland.

    _____

6. a. In Disneyland, I stand around.

    b. In Disneyland, I smile a lot.

    _____

7. a. I usually team up with[1] my friend Goofy.

    b. I usually team up with my friend Minnie.

    (_I team up with only one friend at a time._)

    _____

---

[1]**team up with:** work together as a team

8. a. Together we greet visitors.

   b. We pose for photographs.

   _____

9. I am _____.

   (Write the name of this cartoon animal. Do not write your own name.)

   Who Am I?

   _____ I am a famous cartoon animal. _____

   _____

   _____

   _____

   _____

   _____

   _____

   _____

   _____

   _____

   _____

PART 4 | Writing

Review Questions

Check your understanding of the important points in this chapter by answering the following questions.

Organization

1. What is a paragraph?
2. Can a paragraph discuss more than one topic?
3. What are the three parts of a paragraph?
4. Where do you write the title of a paragraph?
5. What is indenting?
6. What are margins?

Grammar and Capitalization

7. What is a sentence?
8. What is a subject? What is a verb?
9. Do sentences in English always have a subject? What is the only exception to this rule?
10. Do sentences in English always have a verb? Are there any exceptions to this rule?
11. Do sentences in English always have an object?
12. What are six rules for capitalizing words in English?

Sentence Structure

13. What is a simple sentence?
14. What are four simple sentence "formulas"?
15. What kind of ideas do you connect with *and*?
16. When do you use *or*? (Give two answers.)

The Writing Process

Good writing is more than just sitting down and "talking" on a piece of paper. Good writing involves thinking, planning, writing, and revising. You become a good writer by always using these four steps:

1. Prewrite to get ideas and organize them.
2. Write the first draft.
3. Edit: Check and revise your work.
4. Write the final copy.

Step I Prewrite to get ideas—freewriting.

In the prewriting step, you get ideas to write about. Taking notes is one way to gather ideas. You did this kind of prewriting for the paragraph you wrote about a classmate. Another way to get ideas is called **freewriting**. Here is how to do freewriting.

Choose a topic and write it at the top of a piece of paper. Then write whatever sentences come into your mind about the topic. Write horizontally across the paper as you do when you write a letter.

Don't worry about grammar, spelling, or punctuation, and don't worry about putting your ideas into any kind of order. You don't even have to write complete sentences. Just write everything that comes into your mind about your topic. If you can't think of an English word, write it in your own language. The goal is to keep writing without stopping for about ten minutes or until you run out of ideas.

Here is an example of freewriting. It has several mistakes which the writer will correct in a later draft.

> Freewriting About my Grandmother
>
> My grandmother. She was a good cook. The best cook. Every weekend we have a big dinner. With big, big bowls of food. Lots of talking. Everybody in the family there. Every time we eat the same food, but we always love it. Is our favorite meal. She never mad at us. She always defends us when we are in trouble with our parents. One time I picked all the roses in her garden. She not even mad then. Grandmother kind and generous. She gives food to poor people. She never makes them feel bad about taking it. Makes people feel good, just as she made me feel good when I picked all the roses. Thanked me for the beautiful bouquet. Mother really angry. Grandmother always forgives. Forgiving heart.

After you have run out of ideas, edit your freewriting. (Remember that *edit* means to review and change writing in order to improve it.) Read what you have written and choose one main idea for your paragraph. Cross out ideas that aren't related to the one main idea.

In the model, the student decided to write about her grandmother's kindness and forgiving heart. She crossed out the parts about cooking and food.

> Freewriting About my Grandmother
>
> My grandmother. ~~She was a good cook. The best cook. Every weekend we have a big dinner. With big, big bowls of food. Lots of talking. Everybody in the family there. Every time we eat the same food, but we always love it. Is our favorite meal.~~ She never mad at us. She always defends us when we are in trouble with our parents. One time I picked all the roses in her garden. She not mad even then. (Grandmother kind and generous.) She gives food to poor people. She never makes them feel bad about taking it. Makes people feel good, just as she made me feel good when I picked all the roses. Thanked me for the beautiful bouquet. Mother really angry. Grandmother always forgives. Forgiving heart.

Step 2 Write the first draft.

In the second step, you write your paragraph in rough form without worrying too much about errors. This first writing is called the **first draft** or the **rough draft**.

My Grandmother

My grandmother kind and generous. She never mad at us. She always makes people feel good. One time I picked all the roses in her garden. She not mad even then. She made me feel good. Thanked me for the beautiful bouquet. Grandmother gives food to poor people. She never makes them feel bad about taking it. Makes people feel good, just as she made me feel good when I picked all the roses. Grandmother always forgive. Forgiving heart.

Step 3 Edit the first draft.

In the third step, you edit your paragraph. When you edit something, you check it and make changes and corrections. Editing is usually a two-step process.

* In the first step, you check the paragraph as a whole. Is the meaning clear?
* In the second step, you check the paragraph for good form, organization, grammar, punctuation, spelling, and so on.

Step 4 Write the final copy.

In the last step, you write a neat final copy of your paragraph to hand in to your teacher.

Here is the final copy of our model paragraph. The corrections made by the writer include these:

* She crossed out unnecessary sentences.
* She added missing subjects and verbs.
* She moved sentences.
* She changed the ending to match the beginning.

MODEL

Final Copy

> ### My Grandmother
>
> My grandmother is kind and generous. She always makes people feel good. One time I picked all the roses in her garden. She wasn't mad even then. She thanked me for giving her a beautiful bouquet. Grandmother also gives food to poor people. She never makes them feel bad about taking it. She makes them feel good, just as she made me feel good when I picked all the roses. I will always remember my grandmother's kindness and generosity.

Writing Assignment

Write a paragraph about your family or about one person in your family. Use the paragraph "My Grandfather" on pages 21 and 22 or the final copy of "My Grandmother" just above as a model. Practice everything you have learned in this unit.

Use the four steps in the writing process:

Step 1 Prewrite to get ideas.

- Freewrite about your family or about one person in your family for about ten minutes. Read your freewriting and mark it up. Circle ideas that you will use in your paragraph. Cross out ideas that you won't use.

Step 2 Write the first draft.

- Write ROUGH DRAFT at the top of your paper.
- Write the paragraph. Begin it with a sentence that describes your family or family member in general.

  My family is small and close.

  My grandfather is old in years but young in spirit.

  My brother is the irresponsible one in our family.

- Write about eight to ten more sentences about your family or family member. In these sentences, explain what you wrote in your first sentence. How does your family show that they are close? How does your grandfather show that he is young in spirit? In what ways is your brother irresponsible?
- End your paragraph with a sentence that tells how you feel about your family or family member.

  Now we live far from each other, but we will always feel close in our hearts.

  My grandfather will always seem young to me.

  My brother will never grow up.

Step 3 Edit the first draft.

- First, read your paragraph to a classmate, and ask him or her to complete Reader's Response 1B on page 192. Write a second draft.
- Second, check your paragraph against Writer's Self-Check 1B on page 193 to check your own paragraph. Revise your paragraph and write a third draft if necessary.

Step 4 Write the final copy.

- Write a neat final copy of your paragraph to hand in to the teacher. Your teacher may also ask you to hand in your prewriting and your other drafts.

Listing-Order Paragraphs

Chapter Preview

In this chapter, you will write paragraphs that use the listing-order pattern of organization. You will also study and practice:

- the three parts of a paragraph
- listing-order transition signals
- paragraph unity
- simple outlining
- compound sentences
- two common sentence errors

Prewriting Activity: Clustering

Choose a job or profession that you have or would like to have in the future. Here are some possibilities. If you wish, add other jobs that are not on this list.

carpenter	chef	teacher	animal trainer
psychologist	politician	TV news reporter	professional athlete
salesperson	dentist	architect	actor
jockey	waiter	coach	_____
fashion designer	mechanic	model	_____

Discuss the topic with your whole class first, and then work by yourself or in small groups.

1. What characteristics or special abilities does a person need to be successful at the job you have chosen?

   - A **characteristic** is a personal quality that is part of a person's personality. Examples of characteristics are shyness, boldness, patience, honesty, and creativity. A characteristic is something that you *are*.
   - An **ability** is a physical or mental skill. For example, some jobs need people who are good at math, who are good public speakers, or who work well with their hands. An ability is something you *can do*.

Look at the list of some possible characteristics and abilities. Discuss new words, or ask your teacher to tell you other words and expressions that you need.

Characteristics and Abilities		
Adjectives	**Nouns**	**Other**
charismatic	charisma	is good at math
compassionate	compassion	is a good public speaker
creative	creativity	is a leader
dedicated	dedication	likes travel
dependable	dependability	works well with children
diligent	diligence	works well with hands
diplomatic	diplomacy	writes well
fair	fairness	_____
humorous	humor	
intelligent	intelligence	_____
knowledgeable	knowledge	
organized	organization	_____
patient	patience	
self-confident	self-confidence	_____
_____	_____	
_____	_____	
_____	_____	

2. Now think of at least three characteristics and abilities for the job you are writing about. Use the clustering technique described in the next section to help you.

Clustering

Clustering is a prewriting technique that helps you get ideas to write about. Here is how to do clustering.

Begin by writing your chosen job or profession in the center of a piece of paper. Draw a circle around it. Then think about characteristics and abilities necessary for that job, and write down every idea that comes into your mind. Don't stop to worry if the idea is a good one or not. Write words or phrases in circles around the main circle and then connect them to the main circle like in the picture on page 36.

MODEL

Clustering 1

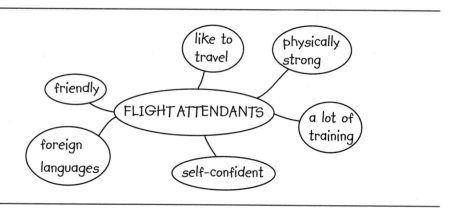

Next, think about the word or phrase in each circle. Try to think of something that illustrates the word or phrase, such as a situation when the person would need a certain characteristic or ability. Also, cross out circles that you don't want.

MODEL

Clustering 2

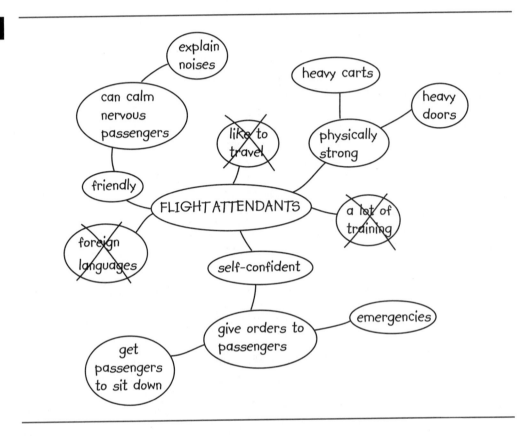

From these clusters, or groups of circles, you can begin to see which ideas to use and which ones to throw away. Use the clusters that have the most circles. Throw away the ones that have few circles because they didn't produce many ideas.

Keep your clustering paper. You will use it later to write a paragraph.

PART 1 | Organization

Organization is one of the most important writing skills. A well-organized paragraph is easy to read and understand because the ideas are in a recognizable pattern. Just as you organize tools on a workbench or clothes in a closet, you also organize sentences in a paragraph. Listing order is a pattern often used in English.

Listing-Order Paragraphs

In a listing-order paragraph, you divide the topic into separate points. Then you discuss one point, and then another point, and then a third point, and so on.

> There are three keys to writing a listing-order paragraph:
>
> 1. Begin with a sentence that names your topic and says it has several points.
> 2. Write about each point separately.
> 3. End with a sentence that reminds your reader about the points you just discussed.

As you read the model paragraph, notice the separate points discussed.

MODEL

Listing-Order Paragraph

Flight Attendants

¹Flight attendants have three important characteristics. ²First of all, flight attendants are friendly. ³They enjoy greeting passengers and making them feel comfortable. ⁴Sometimes passengers are afraid of flying. ⁵A friendly flight attendant can talk to them and help them feel calm. ⁶For example, he or she can explain strange noises made by the aircraft. ⁷Second, flight attendants are self-confident. ⁸They give instructions to passengers, and they must be firm enough so that passengers obey them. ⁹This characteristic is especially important in emergencies. ¹⁰Third, flight attendants are physically strong. ¹¹They push heavy carts of food and drinks up and down the aisles. ¹²They also have to open and close the heavy doors of airplanes. ¹³In short, flight attendants are friendly, self-confident, and strong.

Questions on the Model

1. Look at the title. What is the topic of this paragraph?

2. Look at the first sentence. What does it say about the topic?

3. How many points should the reader look for in this paragraph?

4. List the points here: _____

_____

5. Now look at the last sentence. What information does it repeat?

The Three Parts of a Paragraph

In Chapter 1, you learned that a paragraph has three parts: a topic sentence, supporting sentences, and a concluding sentence. Now we will study each part of a paragraph in more detail.

The Topic Sentence

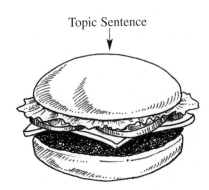

Topic Sentence

The most important sentence in a paragraph is the **topic sentence**. It is called the topic sentence because it tells the reader what the topic of the paragraph is. In other words, it tells the reader what he or she is going to read about. The topic sentence is usually the first sentence in a paragraph. It is the top piece of bread in our paragraph "cheeseburger sandwich."

The Two Parts of a Topic Sentence

A topic sentence has two parts: a **topic** and a **controlling idea**. The topic part names the topic. The controlling idea part tells what the paragraph will say about the topic. It tells the reader: This paragraph will discuss these things—and only these things—about this topic.

For example, the topic of the model paragraph on page 37 is *flight attendants*. What will the paragraph say about flight attendants? The controlling idea tells us: *They have three characteristics*. The paragraph will not tell us about their uniforms, their training, or their duties. It will only discuss three characteristics that flight attendants have.

Here are examples of other topic sentences. The topic in all three examples is the same: *English*. The controlling idea in each says something different about English. From the controlling ideas, can you imagine what the rest of the paragraph will say about English?

English is constantly adding new words.

English borrows words from other languages.

English is necessary for many different jobs.

Usually, the topic comes first and the controlling idea comes second in the topic sentence. However, the controlling idea may come first. In the **a** sentences, the topic is first. In the **b** sentences, the controlling idea is first.

 ┌─Topic─┐┌──────────── Controlling idea ────────────┐
a. English borrows words from other languages.

 ┌──────── Controlling idea ────────┐┌─ Topic ─┐
b. Other languages give words to English.

 ┌─Topic─┐┌──────────── Controlling idea ────────────┐
a. English is necessary for many different jobs.

 ┌──────── Controlling idea ────────┐┌─ Topic ─┐
b. Many different jobs require English.

PRACTICE 1

Two Parts of a Topic Sentence

The following paragraphs show how the controlling idea of a topic sentence controls a paragraph. The topic of all three paragraphs is the same: *beaches*. However, the content of each paragraph is quite different because the controlling idea is different.

Step 1 Find the topic sentence in each paragraph.

Step 2 Draw a circle around the topic and underline the controlling idea. There is one topic sentence in which the topic comes *after* the controlling idea.

The first one has been done as an Example.

Paragraph 1

Beaches

(Beaches) offer different pleasures to different kinds of people. Solitary[1] people can enjoy sunbathing or reading. Social people can usually find someone to talk to or take a walk with. Curious individuals can collect seashells or study the habits of seashore creatures, such as sand crabs or seagulls. Athletes can swim, surf, jog, or play football or volleyball. Indeed, every type of person can find enjoyment at a beach.

---

[1]**solitary:** alone, without companionship

Paragraph 2

Beaches

Beaches are fun in summer and in winter. In summer, you can swim and do many other water sports. If you don't like water sports, you can play beach games or relax on the warm sand. In winter, beaches are less crowded, so they are good places for solitary walks. Also, on a clear winter night, nothing is more fun than sitting with a group of friends around a big bonfire, talking, laughing, and singing. Indeed, a beach is a place to have fun all year.

Paragraph 3

Beaches

Beaches differ in various parts of the world. Thailand has miles of empty beaches. They are beautiful, clean, and uncrowded, even in summer. You can spend the whole afternoon on a beach and not see another person. In Japan, on the other hand, the beaches are very crowded. You can hardly find a place to sit down at the more popular Japanese beaches. The beaches in Northern Europe differ in another way. The water is cold, so most people go to the beach only to sunbathe. Along the French Riviera, the beaches are rocky, not sandy as they are on tropical islands. Each type of beach—empty or crowded, sandy or rocky—has its own special characteristics to enjoy.

Paragraph 4

Beaches

People of all ages have fun at beaches. First, young children love going to a beach. Children love to splash in the water, jump in the waves, and play in the sand. They happily dig holes, fill buckets, and build sand castles all day long. A second group of people who have fun at a beach are teenagers. Teenagers enjoy active water sports, such as surfing, jet skiing, and boardsailing. They also like to just "hang out"[1] at the beach with their friends. Third, senior citizens[2] have a good time at the beach, too. They take long walks along the water's edge or simply relax and enjoy the sunshine. In brief, children, teenagers, and grandparents can all have fun at a beach.

---

[1]**hang out:** relax and socialize (slang)
[2]**senior citizens:** people older than about sixty-five

PRACTICE 2	**A.** Circle the topic and underline the controlling idea in each of the following topic sentences. There is one topic sentence in which the topic comes *after* the controlling idea.
Topic Sentences	

1. (Good roommates) have four characteristics.
2. College students take many kinds of tests.
3. Small cars have several advantages.
4. Big cars are safer than small cars for two reasons.
5. A baseball player must master several skills.
6. Living with your parents has certain advantages.
7. Living with your parents has certain disadvantages.
8. Talent and dedication are two characteristics of Olympic athletes.
9. The Middle East is the birthplace of three major religions.
10. Tokyo has excellent public transportation systems.
11. Tokyo is one of the world's most expensive cities.

B. Read each paragraph. Then choose the best topic sentence and write it on the line provided.

1. _____

_____. First, living in a foreign country helps you learn another language faster than studying it at school. Second, you can learn directly about the history, geography, and culture of a country. Third, you become a more tolerant[3] person because you experience different ways of living. Fourth, living in a foreign country makes you appreciate your own country better.
   a. Living in a foreign country helps you learn.
   b. Everyone should live in a foreign country for a while.
   c. Living in a foreign country has four benefits.

2. _____

_____. Some colleges and universities in the United States are private. Private colleges and universities do not get money from taxes, so they are usually more expensive. Other colleges and universities are public; that is, the citizens of each state pay some of the costs through their taxes. As a result, public colleges are cheaper for students to attend. No matter which type of college you attend—public or private, you can get a good education.
   a. There are two main types of colleges and universities in the United States.
   b. Public colleges and universities get money from taxes.
   c. There are many colleges and universities in the United States.

(continued on next page)

_____

[3] **tolerant:** accepting of differences

3. _____

_____. One reason for choosing a small college is that classes are small. The average class in a small college is twenty students. Another reason is that it is easy to meet with professors. Professors in small colleges have time to help students and are usually happy to do so. In addition, small colleges are friendly, so new students make friends quickly. For these three reasons, small colleges are better than large universities for many students.

   a. Small colleges are friendlier than large universities.
   b. There are several reasons for attending a small college instead of a large university.
   c. You can get an excellent education at a small college.

4. _____

_____. First of all, employers want workers to be dependable. That is, they want workers who come to work every day. Second, employers want workers who are responsible. Can the boss give the worker a project to do and know that it will be done well? Third, employers look for workers who can work well with others. The ability to get along with co-workers is important to the success of a business. To summarize, employers look for dependable, responsible team players.

   a. It is difficult to find good employees these days.
   b. Employers read job applications very carefully.
   c. Employers look for three main qualities in their employees.

C. Write a topic sentence for each of the following paragraphs.

1. _____

_____. Green curry is the hottest Thai curry. People who like very spicy food will enjoy green curry. Red curry is medium hot. It is flavorful, but it doesn't burn your mouth. Yellow curry is the mildest of all. It is usually the choice of people who eat Thai food for the first time. In short, you have three delicious choices when you order Thai curry.

2. _____

_____. First, good teachers know their subject very well. That is, a math teacher has advanced education in mathematics, and an English teacher is an expert in English grammar. Second, good teachers must be good communicators. Being a good communicator means presenting information in ways that students can understand. Third, good teachers are enthusiastic. That is, they are so interested in their subject that they make it fun to learn. To summarize, good teachers have expert knowledge, good communication skills, and contagious[1] enthusiasm.

---

[1] **contagious:** can be transmitted from one person to another person

3. _____

_____. The first type of shopper doesn't like to waste time. She knows what she wants to buy and how much she wants to pay. If the store has what she wants, she buys it and leaves. She is a good kind of customer because she doesn't take too much of a salesperson's time. A second type of shopper comes into a store with a general idea of what she wants, listens to the salesperson's suggestions, tries on a few items, and makes a decision. She is also a good kind of customer. A third kind of shopper has no idea what she wants. She spends two hours trying on one outfit² after another. She takes up a lot of a salesperson's time and sometimes doesn't buy anything. In conclusion, the first two types of shoppers are a salesperson's dream, but the third type is a salesperson's nightmare.

D. Add two different controlling ideas to these topics to make complete topic sentences.

1. Sports

   Different sports are played at different times of the year.

   Each country has its own favorite sport.

2. International students

   _____

   _____

3. Hollywood movies

   _____

   _____

4. Automobile drivers

   _____

   _____

5. Restaurants

   _____

   _____

6. (Your town, city, or country)

   _____

   _____

² **outfit:** set of clothes worn together

Supporting Sentences

Supporting Sentences

The middle sentences of a paragraph are the **supporting sentences**. Supporting sentences explain or prove the idea in the topic sentence. They are the "filling" in a paragraph "sandwich." The supporting sentences are the biggest part of a paragraph, just as the filling is the biggest part of a sandwich.

PRACTICE 3

Supporting Sentences

Work with a partner or in a small group. Discuss possible supporting points for these topic sentences from Practice 2A on page 41. Write your points in the spaces below each sentence. You do not have to write complete sentences.

1. (Good roommates) have four characteristics.
   a. __are neat, tidy__
   b. __are cheerful__
   c. __share housework__
   d. __pay their share of the rent on time__

2. College students take many kinds of tests.
   a. _____
   b. _____
   c. _____

3. Small cars have several advantages.
   a. _____
   b. _____
   c. _____

4. Big cars are safer than small cars for two reasons.
   a. _____
   b. _____

5. A baseball player must master several skills.
   a. _____
   b. _____
   c. _____
   d. _____

6. Living with your parents has certain advantages.
   a. _____
   b. _____
   c. _____

7. Living with your parents has certain disadvantages.

   a. _____

   b. _____

   c. _____

Listing-Order Transition Signals

A **transition signal** is a word or phrase that shows how one idea is related to another idea. In a listing-order paragraph, use transition signals such as *First, Second,* and *Third* to tell your reader that these are main points.

Here are some transition signals that show listing order.

Listing-Order Signals	

1. First,
   First of all,
   Second,
   Third,
   In addition,
   Also,
   Finally,
	2. also
	   , also.

1. Place most listing-order transition signals at the beginning of the sentence, and put a comma after them.

   First, living in a foreign country helps you learn another language faster than studying it at school.

   In addition, small colleges are friendlier, so new students make friends more quickly.

   Also, on a clear winter night, nothing is more fun than sitting with a group of friends around a big bonfire, talking, laughing, and singing.

2. *Also* may come in the middle of a sentence (between the subject and the verb) without a comma or at the end of a sentence with a comma.

   They **also** like to "hang out" at the beach with their friends.

   They like to "hang out" at the beach with their friends, **also**.

PRACTICE 4

*Listing-Order
Transition
Signals*

A. Identify listing-order signals.

Step 1   Circle the listing-order transition signals in the model paragraph about flight attendants on page 37.

Step 2   Copy the transition signals for the three main points of the model paragraph:

Transition signal for the first main point: _____

Transition signal for the second main point: _____

Transition signal for the third main point: _____

Step 3   What other listing-order transition signal can you find in the model paragraph? Write it here: _____

B.   Read the paragraph about human intelligence that follows. Add listing-order signals in the blank spaces, and add commas where they are necessary.

Kinds of Intelligence[1]

There are many kinds of intelligence. (1) _____ there is mathematical-logical intelligence. People with this kind of intelligence become mathematicians, scientists, or engineers. (2) _____ there is linguistic[2] intelligence. People with linguistic intelligence are good at language, so they become poets and writers. We are familiar with these first two kinds of intelligence, but other kinds are not so familiar. There are (3) _____ spatial and musical kinds of intelligence. Spatial intelligence is necessary for architects and artists, and musical intelligence is necessary for musicians. (4) _____ there is kinesthetic[3] intelligence. Athletes and dancers have kinesthetic intelligence. Personal intelligence is a kind of intelligence (5) _____. People with personal intelligence manage people well, so they become leaders of society. In short, there is more than one way to be smart.

Paragraph Unity

Here is an important rule to remember when you write supporting sentences.

> A paragraph must follow the rule of **unity**. All the sentences in a paragraph are about one main idea.

Another way of expressing the rule of unity is to say that all the supporting sentences in a paragraph must be **relevant**. Relevant means "directly related to the main idea." For example, if your paragraph is about your mother's good

---

[1]This paragraph is based on the work of Howard Gardner, a professor at the Harvard Graduate School of Education.
[2]**linguistic:** related to language
[3]**kinesthetic:** related to movement of the human body

cooking, a sentence such as *My sister is also a good cook* is not relevant because the paragraph is about your mother, not your sister. When you write a paragraph, make sure that all of your supporting sentences are relevant. The opposite of *relevant* is *irrelevant*.

PRACTICE 5

Paragraph Unity

Step 1 Read the following paragraphs and locate the topic sentence in each. Circle the topic and underline the controlling idea.

Step 2 In each paragraph, two sentences break the rule of unity. Find these irrelevant sentences, and cross them out.

Paragraph 1

California

^{1}California is a state with every type of geography. ^{2}It has mountains where you can enjoy the winter sports of skiing, snowboarding, and snowshoeing. ^{3}It has deserts where temperatures can reach 110°F (43°C) in the summer. ^{4}It has beaches where you can surf, swim, and fish. ^{5}It has forests where the world's tallest trees grow. ^{6}Finally, it has farmland where a lot of the nation's fruits and vegetables grow. ^{7}California also has Hollywood and Disneyland, which are world-famous centers of entertainment. ^{8}California is a popular place to live, so many people move there every year. ^{9}Indeed, California has it all: mountains, deserts, beaches, and farms.

Paragraph 2

Nurses

^{1}A nurse should have at least five characteristics. ^{2}First, he or she must be a caring person. ^{3}He or she must have genuine concern about sick, injured, frightened people. ^{4}Second, a nurse must be organized. ^{5}If a nurse forgets to give a patient his or her medicine on time, the consequences could be serious. ^{6}Third, a nurse must be calm. ^{7}He or she may have to make a life-and-death decision in an emergency, and a calm person makes better decisions than an excitable one. ^{8}Doctors need to stay calm in emergencies, too. ^{9}In addition, a nurse should be physically strong because nursing requires a lot of hard physical work. ^{10}Finally, a nurse must be intelligent enough to learn subjects ranging from chemistry to psychology and to operate the complex machinery used in hospitals today. ^{11}There is a shortage of nurses today, so they earn good salaries. ^{12}In brief, nursing is a profession for people who are caring, organized, calm, strong, and smart.

The Concluding Sentence

Concluding Sentence

Paragraphs that stand alone (that is, paragraphs that are not part of a longer composition) often have a **concluding sentence** at the end. A concluding sentence closes the paragraph so that the reader is not left expecting more.

1. Sometimes a concluding sentence reminds the reader of the main point by restating the topic sentence in different words.

   > Indeed, a beach is a place to have fun all year.

   > In short, you have three delicious choices when you order Thai curry.

2. Sometimes a concluding sentence summarizes the main points.

   > In short, flight attendants are friendly, self-confident, and strong.

   > To summarize, employers look for dependable, responsible team players.

Writer's Tip

Do NOT introduce a new idea in your concluding sentence. Just review or repeat the ideas you have already discussed. Don't add anything new.

WRONG   Also, flight attendants love to travel.

WRONG   In conclusion, I hope to become a flight attendant some day.

Use a transition signal to tell your reader that this is the end of your paragraph. The following chart lists several conclusion signals. Notice that there is always a comma after conclusion signals.

Conclusion Signals[1]		
To conclude,	**To sum up,**	**In brief,**
In conclusion,	**To summarize,**	**In short,**
	In summary,	**Indeed,**

---

[1] Many teachers tell students not to use the phrases *In conclusion* and *In summary*, but they are listed here because students encounter them in reading.

PRACTICE 6

Concluding Sentences

A. Read the following paragraphs. Then choose the best concluding sentence for it.

Paragraph 1

There are two reasons I love big cities. First of all, big cities are alive 24/7. You can go shopping, see a movie, exercise at a gym, get something to eat, or go roller skating at any time of the day or night. Second, I love big cities because of their anonymity.[2] You can be completely invisible in big cities. No one watches your daily comings and goings.[3] Neighbors don't bother you as long as you don't bother them. You can stay out all night or stay home all day, and no one cares.

  a. To sum up, I love big cities because you can be independent.
  b. In short, big cities attract me because there are so many things to do.
  c. In brief, I like big cities because of their energy and anonymity.

Paragraph 2

There are two reasons I hate big cities. First of all, big cities are full of noise 24/7. You can hear horns honking, traffic roaring, music blaring, and people talking at all hours of the day and night. It is never quiet in a big city. Second, I hate big cities because of their anonymity. No one knows or cares about you. Neighbors who have lived next door to each other for many years don't even know each others' names. You can be very lonely in a big city.

  a. In brief, big cities are noisy, lonely places to live.
  b. In conclusion, I prefer to live in a small town, where it is quieter and people are friendlier.
  c. Also, big cities have a lot of crime.

(continued on next page)

---

[2]**anonymity:** condition of being unknown
[3]**comings and goings:** activities; times when you leave your house and return to it (informal)

B. Write a concluding sentence for the following paragraphs.

Paragraph 1

Goldfish have three characteristics that make them good pets. First of all, goldfish are very quiet. They don't bark, howl, meow, chirp, squawk, screech,[1] or race around the house at night while you and your neighbors are trying to sleep. Second, they are economical. You can buy a goldfish at your local pet store for about 50¢, and a small bowl for it costs less than $3.00. Water is practically free. Also, they eat only a pinch of dried fish food daily, so their food bill is quite low. Third, goldfish are very well behaved. They don't have teeth, so they can't chew your furniture or bite your guests. They don't ever go outside, so they can't dig holes in your garden. In addition, you don't have to spend hours teaching them commands, such as "Sit!" or "Lie down!" _____

_____

Paragraph 2

The island nation of Singapore, the smallest nation in Asia, is one of the best cities in the world to live in and to visit. First of all, Singapore is a very safe city. It has a very low crime rate. Citizens and tourists alike can walk the streets at night without fear. Also, Singapore is very clean. The nation has very strong antilittering laws, so there is almost no litter anywhere. Third, Singaporeans come from many different racial, ethnic, and religious backgrounds, but they live together in peace. Finally, Singapore's economy is one of the healthiest in Asia, so its people enjoy a very high standard of living. _____

_____

C. Choose five topics from Practice 3 on page 44 and write a concluding sentence for each. Try to use a different conclusion signal in each one.

    1. Topic _1_

      To sum up, neatness, cheerfulness, helpfulness, and financial

      responsibility are qualities of good roommates.

---

[1]**bark, howl, meow, chirp, squawk, screech:** different animal sounds

2. Topic ___

_____

_____

3. Topic ___

_____

_____

4. Topic ___

_____

_____

5. Topic ___

_____

_____

6. Topic ___

_____

_____

Outlining

Making an outline is another part of prewriting. Once you get ideas to write about, you need to organize them. An outline helps you do this.

The writer of the two clustering models about flight attendants on pages 35 and 36 chose three characteristics to write about: friendliness, self-confidence, and physical strength. To complete the outline, he added a topic sentence and a concluding sentence.

MODEL

Simple Outline

	Flight Attendants
TOPIC SENTENCE	Flight attendants have three important characteristics.
FIRST MAIN POINT	A. Friendliness
SECOND MAIN POINT	B. Self-confidence
THIRD MAIN POINT	C. Physical strength
CONCLUDING SENTENCE	In short, flight attendants are friendly, self-confident, and strong.

Writer's Tip

When you write an outline, try to make the main points (A, B, C, and so on) the same—all adjectives, all nouns, all verb phrases, or all sentences.

PRACTICE 7

Outlining

Now you try it. Make an outline from the Prewriting Activity: Clustering that you did at the beginning of the chapter (pages 34–36). Use the following form for your outline.

Step 1 Look at your final cluster of circles. Mark ideas that seem useful for this topic, and cross out ideas that don't seem useful. Try to find three main points. Label them A, B, C.

Step 2 Write a topic sentence and a concluding sentence.

Title: _____

TOPIC SENTENCE _____

FIRST MAIN POINT   A. _____

SECOND MAIN POINT   B. _____

THIRD MAIN POINT   C. _____

CONCLUDING SENTENCE _____

Try It Out! Write a paragraph from the outline you wrote in Practice 7. Use the model paragraph on page 37 as a guide. (You have already completed Step 1 in the writing process, Prewriting.)

Step 2 **Write the first draft.**

- Write ROUGH DRAFT at the top of your paper.
- Follow your outline.
- Add details that show when each characteristic or ability is used or why it is important. Write two or three sentences for each main point.
- Introduce each main point with a listing-order transition signal.

Step 3 **Edit the first draft.**

- Edit your paragraph with a partner as you have done in Chapter 1. Use Reader's Response 2A and Writer's Self-Check 2A on pages 194 and 195.

Step 4 **Write the final copy.**

- Write a neat final copy to hand in to your teacher. Your teacher may also ask you to hand in your prewriting, your outline, and your other drafts.

PART 2 | Sentence Structure

Compound Sentences

In Chapter 1, you learned about simple sentences. Another kind of sentence is a **compound sentence**.

> A **compound sentence** is two simple sentences connected by a comma and a coordinating conjunction.

This is the basic formula for a compound sentence:

Simple sentence	,	COORDINATING CONJUNCTION	simple sentence.

These are compound sentences:

Simple Sentence	Coordinating Conjunction	Simple Sentence
My family goes camping every summer,	and	we usually have fun.
Last year we went camping at Blue Lake,	but	we had a terrible time.
Next year we will go to the beach,	or	perhaps we will stay at home.
We want to buy a house soon,	so	we need to save money.

Command sentences can also be compound. Remember that the subject "you" is not expressed in commands.

(~~You~~) Come visit us again soon,	and	~~you~~ bring your family with you.
(~~You~~) Have a good time,	but	~~you~~ don't stay out too late.

Here are three important points to know about compound sentences:

1. A comma and a coordinating conjunction connect the two halves of a compound sentence.
2. There are seven coordinating conjunctions in English: *for, and, nor, but, or, yet,* and *so.* Remember them by the phrase "fan boys." In this book, you will practice four of them: *and, but, or,* and *so.*
3. Don't confuse a compound sentence with a simple sentence that has a compound verb. The first sentence in each of the following pairs of sentences is simple and doesn't need a comma. The second one is compound and requires a comma.

		"Formulas"
Simple sentence with compound verb	My family goes camping every summer and usually has fun.	S V V
Compound sentence	My family goes camping every summer, and we usually have fun.	S V, and S V
Simple sentence with compound verb	Last year we went camping but had a terrible time.	S V V
Compound sentence	Last year we went camping, but everyone had a terrible time.	S V, but S V
Simple sentence with compound verb	Next year we will go to the beach or perhaps stay at home.	S V V
Compound sentence	Next year we will go to the beach, or perhaps we will stay at home.	S V, or S V

PRACTICE 8

Simple versus Compound Sentences

A. Identify simple and compound sentences.

Step 1 Analyze each sentence in the following paragraphs. Underline the subjects with one line and the verbs with two lines.

Step 2 Circle coordinating conjunctions (*and, but, or, so*) that separate two simple sentences.

Step 3 Write *simple* or *compound* in the space to the left of each sentence, and write the formula for each: SV, *and* SV, SVV, *or* SSV, and so on.

Step 4 Add a comma to compound sentences.

   simple   SV   1. The summers were hot and humid in my childhood hometown.

  compound SV, so SSV 2. Every evening it was too hot to sleep, so my sisters and I played outside until dark.

_____ _____ 3. Our parents sat in chairs on the grass and watched us play our children's games.

_____ _____ 4. We played games such as hide-and-seek and tag or we just sat on the grass and told stories.

_____ _____ 5. We also caught fireflies.[1]

_____ _____ 6. We put the fireflies into a glass jar and our father punched air holes in the metal lid.

[1]**fireflies:** insects with tails that shine in the dark

_____ _____ 7. My sisters were afraid of most bugs but they loved fireflies.

_____ _____ 8. We usually went to bed at nine o'clock but we stayed up until ten on really warm evenings.

_____ _____ 9. Around ten o'clock our mother and father told us to come inside.

_____ _____ 10. "Come inside now but leave the fireflies outside, please," our mother always said.

B. Identify simple and compound sentences in a paragraph.

Step 1 Analyze each sentence in the following paragraph. Underline the subjects with one line and the verbs with two lines.

Step 2 Write *simple* or *compound* in the numbered spaces.

Step 3 Then write the formula for each sentence.

Step 4 Add commas wherever they are needed. (You should add seven commas.)

Teenagers

¹Teenagers find many ways to drive their parents crazy. ²First, they dye their hair purple, or they shave their heads bald.² ³They also tattoo their skin and wear rings in their noses. ⁴In addition they spend hours at the shopping mall and on the phone. ⁵They have time to watch TV but they don't have time

(continued on next page)

<hr>

²**bald:** no hair at all

to do their homework. ⁶Also they're always too busy to clean up¹ their rooms but they're never too busy to clean out² the refrigerator by eating everything in it. ⁷Finally they are old enough to drive but too young to pay for gas. ⁸They are usually broke³ so they always return the family car with an empty gas tank. ⁹It's hard to be a teenager but it's even harder to be the parent of one.

1. __simple__　　__SV__　　　　6. _____　　_____
2. __compound__　__SV, or SV__　　7. _____　　_____
3. _____　_____　　　　8. _____　　_____
4. _____　_____　　　　9. _____　　_____
5. _____　_____

Coordinating Conjunctions: *and, but, or, so*

In compound sentences, *and, but, or,* and *so* have these meanings:

And connects two sentences with similar ideas. The sentences can be positive or negative.

> My roommate is an art student, **and** her boyfriend plays in a rock band.

> She doesn't like rock music, **and** he doesn't like art.

Writer's Tip

Remember to use *or*, not *and*, in a negative simple sentence. To refresh your memory, turn back to Chapter 1, page 23.

> He doesn't like art **or** classical music.

But connects two sentences with contrasting or opposite ideas.

> She likes classical music, **but** she doesn't like rock.

> She likes country music, **but** he hates it.

Or connects two sentences that express alternatives or choices.

> Every Friday night, they go to a classical concert, **or** they visit an art gallery.

> Every Saturday night, he practices with his band, **or** they go to hear a rock concert.

---

¹**clean up:** make clean and neat by removing things that make it look messy
²**clean out:** make clean and neat by removing things; the slang expression *clean out* can mean *remove everything* as in *The robbers cleaned out the cash drawer.*
³**broke:** having no money

So connects a reason and a result.

Reason	Result
They both like jazz,	**so** they go to jazz concerts together.
He works a lot,	**so** they don't go out very often.

PRACTICE 9

And, but, or, and so in Simple and Compound Sentences

Fill in the blanks with one of these four coordinating conjunctions: *and, but, or, so.* You may want to review the use of *and, but, or,* and *so* in simple sentences on page 53 before you do this exercise.

1. The waitress said, "Today we have two specials: fried chicken __and__ meatloaf."[4]
2. I ordered meatloaf, _____ my friend ordered fried chicken.
3. After an hour, the waitress came back to our table and said, "I made a mistake. We don't have chicken _____ meatloaf."
4. I wanted to leave the restaurant immediately, _____ my friend wanted to stay.
5. He ordered a hamburger _____ french fries, _____ I didn't order anything.
6. My new neighbors are vegetarians, _____ they don't eat meat.
7. They don't eat meat _____ chicken, _____ sometimes they eat a little fish.
8. I wanted to be friendly, _____ I invited them to my house for dinner.
9. They came _____ brought their young son.
10. He is just a baby, _____ he can't talk yet.
11. They don't drink coffee _____ tea, _____ I served lemonade with our meal.
12. For dessert, I offered them a choice of chocolate cake _____ apple pie.
13. The husband wanted both cake and pie, _____ the wife didn't want either.

PRACTICE 10

Writing Compound Sentences

A. Write compound sentences.

Step 1 Connect the two simple sentences in each pair to make a compound sentence. Connect them with *and, but, or,* or *so*—whichever best fits the meaning. There may be more than one possible choice.

Step 2 Add a comma to each sentence.

1. Canada has two official languages. Everything is printed in both English and French.

   Canada has two official languages, so everything is printed in both

   English and French.

(continued on next page)

---

[4]**meatloaf:** dish made from ground meat, breadcrumbs, egg, and spices and baked in a pan like a loaf of bread

2. There are several hundred languages in the world. Not all of them have a written form.

_____

_____

3. Chinese is spoken by more people. English is spoken in more countries.

_____

_____

4. Russian is the third most spoken language in the world. Spanish is the fourth.

_____

_____

5. There are about one million words in English. Most people use only about ten thousand of them.

_____

_____

6. Chinese has many different dialects.[1] Chinese people cannot always understand each other.

_____

_____

7. French used to be the language of international diplomacy. Now it is English.

_____

_____

8. International companies are growing. They will soon need more bilingual workers.

_____

_____

9. Young people should know a second language. They will be at a disadvantage in the international job market.

_____

_____

---

[1] **dialects:** variations of the standard language

B. Make compound sentences by adding a second simple sentence to each item.

1. My brother and I look like twins, but   <u>our personalities are very different</u> .

2. We are both medium tall, and _____

   _____.

3. He is an extrovert,[2] but _____

   _____.

4. I am younger, so _____

   _____.

5. Our mother used to tell us, "Stop fighting, or _____

   _____.

6. We fought a lot as children, but now _____

   _____.

7. We married two sisters, so _____

   _____.

Two Sentence Errors: Run-ons and Comma Splices

Two sentence errors that writers sometimes make are **run-ons** and **comma splices**. These mistakes happen most often when the two sentences are related in meaning.

- A run-on is two simple sentences incorrectly joined with no coordinating conjunction and no comma.

  WRONG: My roommate wants to win the Tour de France someday he spends hours riding his bicycle.

  WRONG: Write your signature on the line print your name below it.

- A comma splice is two simple sentences incorrectly joined with a comma alone.

  WRONG: My roommate wants to win the Tour de France someday, he spends hours riding his bicycle.

  WRONG: Write your signature on the line, print your name below it.

There are two ways to fix these errors.

1. Separate the sentences with a period.

  RIGHT: My roommate wants to win the Tour de France someday**.** He spends hours riding his bicycle.

  RIGHT: Write your signature on the line. Print your name below it.

---

[2]**extrovert:** someone who is active and confident and who enjoys being with other people

OR

2. Add (or keep) the comma and add a coordinating conjunction.

<table>
<tr><td>RIGHT:</td><td>My roommate wants to win the Tour de France someday, **so** he spends hours riding his bicycle.</td></tr>
<tr><td>RIGHT:</td><td>Write your signature on the line, **and** print your name below it.</td></tr>
</table>

PRACTICE 11

Fixing Run-ons and Comma Splices

Find and correct the sentence errors.

Step 1 Put an X in the space next to the sentences that are comma splices or run-ons.

Step 2 Correct the sentences that you marked. Use either method 1 or 2 (from pages 59–60) to correct them.

  _X_   1. Some people like cats, others prefer dogs.

           Some people like cats. Others prefer dogs.

  OR   _Some people like cats, and others prefer dogs._

  OR   _Some people like cats, but others prefer dogs._

—— 2. Kittens are cute, they like to play.

—— 3. Dogs are good companions, and they can also protect you.

—— 4. It's acceptable for dogs to bark at strangers they shouldn't bite them, however.

_____

_____

—— 5. Lions are also good protectors, but they eat too much.

_____

_____

—— 6. Penguins[1] always wear tuxedos,[2] they are good pets for people who like to go to fancy parties.

_____

_____

—— 7. A pet elephant can fan you with his ears and spray you with his trunk,[3] you won't need air-conditioning or a shower.

_____

_____

—— 8. Goats eat lots of grass, so you will never have to cut your lawn.[4]

_____

_____

—— 9. A giraffe can reach things on high shelves, it can see over the heads of people at parades.

_____

_____

—— 10. Keep a boa constrictor[5] as a pet if you enjoy being alone then no one will ever visit you.

_____

_____

---

[1]**penguins:** birds that live in Antarctica. They stand upright and have black and white feathers.
[2]**tuxedos:** men's fancy black suits, worn on very formal occasions such as weddings
[3]**trunk:** elephant's long nose
[4]**lawn:** grass in a garden
[5]**boa constrictor:** very large snake

Try It Out!   Step 1 Combine the sentences in each group to make one sentence. Some of your sentences will be simple, and some will be compound. There may be more than one possible correct way to combine each group.

Step 2 Write the sentences as a paragraph. Add listing-order transition signals to each main point and a conclusion signal to the concluding sentence. (*Hint*: There are three main points.)

The "Weaker" Sex

1. It is often said that women are the weaker sex, but women are actually superior to men in several ways. (Don't change this sentence.)

2. a. Women live longer than men.
   b. Women stay healthier than men.
   c. They do this in all countries of the world.

3. a. This difference starts at birth.
   b. This difference continues until old age.

4. a. On the average, women live seven years longer than men.
   b. They do this in the United States.

5. a. There are 105 boys to every 100 girls at birth.
   b. There are twice as many women as men at age 80.
      (Use *but*.)

6. a. Women are better than men at things.
   b. These things involve the five senses.
      (Change *these things* to *that*.)

7. a. Women have a sharper sense of taste.
   b. Women have a sharper sense of smell.

8. a. Men are physically stronger than women.
   b. Women are mentally stronger.

9. a. For example, more men than women had emotional problems.
   b. This happened during bombing attacks on London.
   c. This happened in World War II.

10. Do you still believe that women are "the weaker sex"? (Don't change this sentence.)

Paragraph

The "Weaker" Sex

It is often said that women are the weaker sex, but women are actually superior to men in several ways. Women live longer and stay healthier than men in all countries of the world.

_____

_____

_____

_____

_____

_____

_____

_____

_____

_____

_____

_____

PART 3 | Writing

Review Questions

Check your understanding of the important points in this chapter by answering the following questions.

Organization

1. What is clustering? How do you do it?
2. What is listing order?
3. What are the three parts of a paragraph?
4. What are the two parts of a topic sentence?
5. What does the controlling idea do?
6. What are transition signals? What are some listing-order transition signals?
7. What is unity in a paragraph?
8. What are two ways to write a concluding sentence?
9. What is an outline? How does an outline help writers?

Sentence Structure

10. What is the formula for a compound sentence?
11. Where do you put a comma in a compound sentence?
12. What are two common sentence errors?
13. What are two ways to correct them?

Writing Assignment

Choose one of the topics from Practice 2A on page 41 or from Practice 2D on page 43 and write a paragraph. Use listing order to organize your ideas. Follow the steps in the writing process.

Step 1 Prewrite to get ideas.

- Make a list to get main ideas and details about your topic.
- Edit your list. Choose two to four main points.
- Make an outline. Make a form for yourself like the one on page 52. Your outline should include all three parts of a paragraph: topic sentence, supporting sentences (main points), and concluding sentence.

Step 2 Write the first draft.

- Write ROUGH DRAFT at the top of your paper.
- Use a listing-order signal to introduce each new main point. Also, use a conclusion signal with the concluding sentence.
- Write two or three additional sentences to explain each main point.
- Include at least three compound sentences somewhere in your paragraph.

Step 3 Edit the first draft.

- Edit your paragraph with a partner as you have done in Chapter 1. Use the Reader's Response 2B and Writer's Self-Check 2B on pages 196 and 197.

Step 4 Write the final copy.

- Write a neat final copy of your paragraph to hand in to the teacher. Your teacher may also ask you to hand in your prewriting, your outline, and your other drafts.

Giving Instructions

Chapter Preview
  Prewriting Activity: Listing

Part 1: Organization
  "How To" Paragraphs
  Listing and Outlining

Part 2: Sentence Structure
  Independent and Dependent Clauses
  Complex Sentences
  Sentence Errors: Fragments
  Summary: Three Types of Sentences

Part 3: Capitalization and Punctuation
  Capitalization: Four More Rules
  Commas: Four Rules

Part 4: Writing

Chapter Preview

In this chapter, you will write paragraphs that explain how to do something or how to make something. You will also study and practice:

- time order and time-order signals
- complex sentences with time clauses
- fragments (a sentence error)
- four new capitalization rules
- one new comma rule

Prewriting Activity: Listing

Work with a group of at least three students or with the entire class.

1. Look at the picture of the messy house after a party on page 65.

2. Make a list of all the things you should do to clean it up. Write down every idea. Don't worry about putting the ideas in order. You will do that later.

3. After your group has finished listing, your teacher may ask you to share your list with other groups. Keep your list. You will use it later to write a paragraph.

Listing: How to Clean Up After a Party

_____

_____

_____

_____

_____

_____

_____

_____

_____

_____

_____

_____

_____

_____

_____

PART 1 | Organization

"How To" Paragraphs

In this chapter, you will learn to write a paragraph that gives instructions. This kind of paragraph is sometimes called a "how to" paragraph because it explains how to do something or how to make something—how to change a flat tire or how to perform a science experiment, for example.

There are four keys to writing clear "how to" paragraphs.

1. Begin with a topic sentence that names the topic and says the paragraph will give instructions about it.

2. Divide the instructions into a series of steps. For some topics, you will put the steps in order by time and use time-order transition signals to show the order.

   First, do this. **Next,** do that.

   For other topics, you can use listing order.

3. Explain each step one by one.

4. Use transition signals to introduce each new step.

Keep these four keys in your mind as you read the model paragraph.

MODEL

"How To" Paragraph

How to Have a Successful Garage Sale

¹Prepare ahead in order to have a successful garage sale. ²First, collect used items in good condition. ³These items can be clothes, toys, books, dishes, lamps, furniture, TVs, pictures, and sporting goods. ⁴Clean everything well and store it in your garage until the day of the sale. ⁵Next, decide on a day and time for your sale. ⁶Third, decide on the prices, and mark a price on each item. ⁷If you are not sure how much to charge, check the prices at other garage sales in your community.

(continued on next page)

⁸Fourth, make signs advertising the date, time, and address of your sale, and put them up around your neighborhood. ⁹Then get some change from the bank. ¹⁰Get at least twenty dollars in one-dollar bills, a roll of quarters, and a roll of dimes. ¹¹Finally, get up early on the morning of the sale, and arrange the items on tables in your driveway and in your garage. ¹²After that, sit back and wait for your customers to arrive. ¹³Be prepared to bargain! ¹⁴If you follow all of these steps, your garage sale will be a great success.

Questions on the Model

1. What is the topic of the model paragraph?
2. Which sentence tells you the topic? What is this sentence called?
3. How many main steps does the paragraph explain?
4. Circle the transition signals that introduce each main step.
5. Does this paragraph use time order or listing order to organize the steps?

Writer's Tip

Notice that many of the verbs in the model are commands: *collect, clean, store, decide, mark,* and so on. Use the command verb form to give instructions.

Topic and Concluding Sentences for "How To" Paragraphs

The topic part of a topic sentence for a "how to" paragraph names the topic. The controlling idea part tells your readers that they will learn how to do or make something. In the model paragraph, the topic sentence names the topic: *a garage sale*. It also tells what your paragraph will tell your reader about garage sales: *how to prepare in order to have a successful one*.

Here are other examples of topic sentences for "how to" paragraphs. Notice that they use expressions such as *by taking these steps, if you follow my advice*, and *follow these instructions*. These expressions tell your reader that this is a "how to" paragraph.

> Anyone can change a flat tire by taking these steps.
>
> It's easy to soothe a crying baby if you follow my advice.
>
> Follow these instructions to make delicious pizza.

The concluding sentence of a "how to" paragraph mentions the topic again to remind the reader what the paragraph was about.

> In no time at all, your flat tire will be repaired, and you will be on your way again.
>
> If you follow these four steps, your baby will fall asleep within five minutes.
>
> You now have a delicious pizza to enjoy.

PRACTICE 1

Topic Sentences for "How To" Paragraphs

Work with a partner or a small group.

A. Complete topic sentences for "how to" paragraphs by filling in the blanks.

1. It's easy to <u>write a paragraph</u> if you <u>follow the four steps in the writing process</u>.

2. It is simple to _____ if you _____.

3. Anyone can learn to _____ if he or she _____ _____.

4. Follow these instructions to _____.

5. Make/Draw/Write/Cook a perfect _____ by following these steps.

B. Now write three original topic sentences for "how to" paragraphs. Use some of the topic suggestions that are listed, or think of other topics that you might want to use later when you write your own "how to" paragraph.

1. _____

_____

2. _____

_____

3. _____

_____

Topic Suggestions

Get an A in English

Get an F in English

Meet people in a new place

Learn a new language

Get the job of your dreams

Check the oil in a car

Change a flat tire

Study for a test

Avoid studying for a test

Get on a horse

Raise a happy child

Raise a spoiled child

Catch a fish

Train a falcon/hunting dog/parrot

Make pizza/baklava/borscht/nachos (or any special food)

Make a piñata

Decorate an egg

Use chopsticks

Play a children's game

Time-Order Signals

In a "how to" paragraph, you can use either **listing-order signals** or **time-order signals**. You learned about listing-order signals in Chapter 2. Notice that many listing-order and time-order signals are the same.

• If the steps in your instructions must be in a specific order (such as in the model paragraph about how to have a successful garage sale), use time-order signals.

• If the order doesn't matter, use listing-order signals.

Listing-Order Signals	Time-Order Signals	

1. First,
    First of all,
    Second,
    Third,
    In addition,
    Also,
    Finally,
	1. First,
	    First of all,
	    Second,
	    Third,
	    Next,
	    After that,
	    Then
	    Finally,
		2. before a test
		    in the morning
		    during a flight

1. These transition signals usually appear at the beginning of a sentence, followed by a comma. *Then* is an exception. Do not put a comma after *then*.

    First, make the pizza dough.

    Then add 2 cups of flour.

2. You can use any time expression as a time-order signal. You can put time expressions such as these almost anywhere in a sentence.

    Before a big test, get a good night's sleep.

    In the morning, be sure to eat breakfast.

    Drink a lot of water **during a flight.**

Writer's Tip

Do not put a transition signal at the beginning of every sentence in a "how to" paragraph. A paragraph with too many transition signals is just as confusing to the reader as a paragraph with none! Use a transition signal with important steps, not with every step.

PRACTICE 2

Listing Order or Time Order?

In a small group or with the whole class, think about each of the following topics for "how to" paragraphs. Which topics require time order, and which topics can use listing order? Write *TO* (Time Order) or *LO* (Listing Order) in the space next to each topic.

__TO__ 1. How to study for a test

__LO__ 2. How to get fit

_____ 3. How to change the oil in a car

_____ 4. How to meet people in a new place

_____ 5. How to impress your boss

(continued on next page)

_____ 6. How to learn a new language

_____ 7. How to shop economically

_____ 8. How to write a paragraph

_____ 9. How to get a driver's license

_____ 10. How to prepare for an earthquake

PRACTICE 3

Transition Signals

Each of the following groups of sentences includes a topic sentence and several steps.

Step 1 Decide which sentence is the topic sentence. Give it the number "1."

Step 2 Decide which three of the four groups should be in time order. Number the steps in these three paragraphs in the correct time order. (The remaining group of sentences will be listing order.)

Step 3 Choose two groups of sentences and write each group as a paragraph. Write the paragraphs on a separate piece of paper.

- Copy the title and topic sentence. The topic sentence is the first sentence of the paragraph, so remember to indent it.
- Copy the remaining sentences in order.
- Add a transition signal to some (not all) steps.

1. **How to Prevent Jet Lag**[1]

   __1__ Frequent flyers recommend these steps to prevent jet lag.

   _____ Don't drink alcohol or coffee during the flight.

   _____ Go to bed early your first night in the new time zone.

   __2__ Eat a high-carbohydrate[2] meal before your flight.

   _____ Don't nap[3] during the day when you arrive.

Paragraph

_____ How to Prevent Jet Lag _____

_____

_____ Frequent flyers recommend these steps to prevent jet lag. First of all,

eat a high-carbohydrate meal before your flight. Second, . . .

_____

_____

_____

-----

[1]**jet lag:** tiredness caused by travel through several time zones
[2]**carbohydrate:** foods such as rice, potatoes, and breads
[3]**nap:** sleep for a short time

2. **How to Drive Your Teacher Crazy**

_____ It's easy to drive your teacher crazy if you follow these simple directions.

_____ Yawn and look at your watch as often as possible during the class.

_____ Make a lot of noise when you enter the classroom.

_____ At least five minutes before the end of class, slam your books shut and stare at the door.

_____ Always come to class at least five minutes late.

3. **How to Plan a Family Vacation**

_____ Consider the interests and abilities of everyone in the family.

_____ Decide how long you can be away from home.

_____ Decide how much money you can spend.

_____ Planning a family vacation takes careful thought.

_____ Find out when everyone can take time off from school and jobs.

_____ When you have the answers to all of these questions, visit a travel agency.

4. **How to Wax a Car**

Note: In this group, some sentences belong together as part of the same step. When you write this paragraph, do not use transition signals with every sentence. Use them only in front of a new step, which are marked with an asterisk (*).

_____ Keep your car looking great by following these easy steps to wax it.

_____ After you have put wax on the entire car, start to remove it, section by section.

_____ *Wash and dry the car thoroughly.

_____ Use a soft towel to remove the wax in the same order that you applied it.

_____ Work on one section at a time, and rub the wax into the car in small circles.

_____ *Park your car in a cool, shady spot.

_____ *Polish the car with a soft cloth to remove any remaining wax and to bring out the shine.

_____ *Dip a damp sponge into a can of wax.

Listing and Outlining

In Chapter 1, you got ideas by freewriting. In Chapter 2, you got ideas by clustering. The **listing** activity that you did at the beginning of this chapter is another way to get ideas. In listing, you make a list of every word or phrase that comes into your mind when you think about a topic. As with freewriting and clustering, you don't stop to wonder if an idea is good or if your spelling or grammar is correct. You just keep writing down words in a list until you run out of ideas.

Here is the list made by the writer of the model paragraph on how to have a successful garage sale.

MODEL

Listing

How to Have a Successful Garage Sale	
collect used things in good condition	people don't buy broken or dirty things
—clothes	get change from the bank
—toys	ask your friends to help
—books	decide on the prices
—old dishes	put a price on each item
store them in the garage	buy price tags
clean everything	make sure everything is clean
clean the garage	wash and iron the clothes
arrange items on tables	advertise
borrow tables	try to have it on a sunny day
make signs	decide on a day and time
put them around the neighborhood	be prepared to bargain

After you have made a list, the next step is to edit the list. Decide what you want to include in your final paragraph and what you want to omit.

Notice how the writer edited his list.

1. He crossed out unimportant and repeated items.
2. He numbered the main steps in order by time.

MODEL
Edited List

How to Have a Successful Garage Sale

1. collect used things in ~~people don't buy broken or~~
   good condition ~~dirty things~~
   —clothes   9. get change from the bank
   —toys   ~~ask your friends to help~~
   —books   5. decide on the prices
   —old dishes   6. put a price on each item
3. store them in the garage   ~~buy price tags~~
2. clean everything   ~~make sure everything is clean~~
   ~~clean the garage~~   ~~wash and iron the clothes~~
10. arrange items on tables   ~~advertise~~
    ~~borrow tables~~   ~~try to have it on a sunny day~~
7. make signs   4. decide on a day and time
8. put them around the   11. be prepared to bargain
   neighborhood

The next step is to make an outline. To make a simple outline, change the numbers to capital letters (A, B, C, D, and so on), write a topic sentence at the beginning, and add a concluding sentence at the end.

Here is the student's completed outline.

MODEL
Simple Outline
TITLE
TOPIC SENTENCE

How to Have a Successful Garage Sale

It's easy to have a successful garage sale if you prepare for it ahead of time.

A. Collect used things in good condition
B. Clean the items and store them in the garage
C. Decide on a day and time for your sale
D. Decide on the prices and mark a price on each item
E. Make signs to advertise
F. Put signs around the neighborhood
G. Get change from a bank
H. Arrange items on tables in your driveway or yard
I. Be prepared to bargain

CONCLUDING SENTENCE   If you follow all of these steps, your garage sale will be a great success.

PRACTICE 4

Simple Outlining

Write an outline from the list you made at the beginning of this chapter on how to clean up after a party.

Step 1 Edit the list by crossing out repeated ideas or ideas that don't fit.

Step 2 Decide whether to use time order or listing order.

Step 3 Put the steps in order.

Step 4 Add a title, a topic sentence, and a concluding sentence.

Try It Out!

Write a paragraph about how to clean up a house after a party. You have already completed Step 1 (Prewriting). Now continue with the writing process.

Step 2 Write the first draft.

- Write ROUGH DRAFT at the top of your paper.
- Follow your outline.
- Use transition signals to introduce some steps.
- If you wish, add other sentences to explain each step in more detail.

Step 3 Edit the first draft.

- Edit your paragraph with a partner as you have done in previous chapters. Use the Reader's Response 3A and Writer's Self-Check 3A on pages 198 and 199.

Step 4 Write the final copy.

- Write a neat final copy of your paragraph to hand in to your teacher. Your teacher may also ask you to hand in your prewriting, your outline, and your other drafts.

PART 2 | Sentence Structure

In Chapters 1 and 2, you learned about simple and compound sentences. A third kind of sentence is a **complex sentence**. Before we study these, let's learn about clauses.

Independent and Dependent Clauses

A **clause** is a group of words that contains a subject and a verb. There are two kinds of clauses in English: **independent clauses** and **dependent clauses**.

Independent Clause	Dependent Clause
S V	S V
It rained.	. . . because it rained . . .

1. An **independent clause** has one SV pair and expresses a complete thought. *Independent clause* is just another name for a simple sentence.

   S   V
   Paris has excellent art museums.

   S   V
   We finished our homework.

2. A **dependent clause** is an independent clause with a subordinating word, such as *because, after,* and *when,* added to the beginning of it.

   SUBORDINATING
   WORD   S   V
   . . . **because** Paris has excellent art museums . . .

   SUBORDINATING
   WORD   S   V
   . . . **after**   we finished our homework . . .

   A dependent clause does not express a complete thought, so it is not a sentence by itself. It is only half of a sentence. It MUST be joined to an independent clause. Together, the two clauses express a complete thought.

   ┌────── INDEPENDENT CLAUSE ──────┐┌────── DEPENDENT CLAUSE ──────┐
   Art students should visit Paris because it has excellent art museums.

   ┌────── DEPENDENT CLAUSE ──────┐┌────── INDEPENDENT CLAUSE ──────┐
   After we finished our homework, we watched TV for a while.

   ## Adverb Subordinators

   There are many subordinating words that can make a dependent clause. In this chapter, we will study **adverb subordinators**. We call them adverb subordinators because they introduce dependent clauses that act like adverbs. That is, they answer the questions *when?, why?, where?,* and so on.

Certain adverb subordinators introduce time clauses. Here are some common **time subordinators**.

Time Subordinators	
after	I will go straight to bed **after** I finish writing this paragraph.
as soon as	She felt better **as soon as** she took the medicine.
before	Wait for a green light **before** you cross a street.
since	It has been a year **since** I left home.
until	We can't leave the room **until** everyone finishes the test.
when	Where were you **when** I called?
whenever	**Whenever** I don't sleep well, I feel sick the next day.
while	My neighbors were having a party **while** I was trying to sleep.

Caution!

A few time subordinators are also prepositions. Prepositions are followed by nouns. Subordinators are followed by subject-verb combinations

after my accident (*preposition*)

after I had an accident (*subordinator*)

before class (*preposition*)

before class begins (*subordinator*)

until ten o'clock (*preposition*)

until the bell rings (*subordinator*)

Writer's Tip

In addition to time-order transition signals, such as *first, next, after that*, and so on, you can use time clauses to show time order.

Before you start writing, look over the test.

After you have answered the easy questions, go back and work on the hard ones.

PRACTICE 5

Independent and Dependent Clauses

Identify independent and dependent clauses.

Step 1 Write *IC* (independent clause) or *DC* (dependent clause) in the space to the left of each group of words.

Step 2 If it is an IC, add a period. If it is a DC, circle the time subordinator.

    IC   1. I take a walk around the block.
    DC   2. (Before) I go to work
    ____ 3. The exercise wakes up my body and clears my mind
    ____ 4. It's hard to do this in the winter
    ____ 5. When I go to work
    ____ 6. It is still dark
    ____ 7. After I get home from work
    ____ 8. It is dark again
    ____ 9. I can always take a walk on weekends, even in the winter
    ____ 10. When it is raining, of course
    ____ 11. I never go out
    ──── 12. On rainy days, as soon as the alarm clock rings
    ──── 13. I turn over and go back to sleep

Complex Sentences

Now that you know about dependent and independent clauses, let's learn about complex sentences.

A **complex sentence** has one independent clause and one (or more) dependent clauses.

- When the dependent clause begins with an adverb subordinator, the clauses can usually be in any order.

    We ran for shelter as soon as it started to rain.

    As soon as it started to rain, we ran for shelter.

- If the independent clause is first, don't use a comma.
- If the dependent clause is first, put a comma after it.

<table>
<tr><td>

PRACTICE 6

*Complex
Sentences
with Time
Subordinators*

</td><td>

A. Analyze these complex sentences.

Step 1 Underline the independent clauses with a <u>solid line</u> and the dependent clauses with a <u>broken line</u>.

Step 2 Draw a circle around the time subordinator.

Step 3 Add a comma if one is needed.

</td></tr>
</table>

1. (After) we won the lottery last year, my wife and I decided to take a trip.

2. We were very excited when we won.

3. After we got our first payment we started planning a trip to Italy.

4. Before we left on our trip we wrote to our cousins in Rome and told them our plans.

5. As soon as they received our letter they called and invited us to stay with them.

6. They were waiting at the airport when we arrived.

7. They waited outside while the Italian officials checked our passports and luggage.

8. Finally, after we got our suitcases they drove us to their home.

9. As soon as we arrived at their apartment they wanted to feed us.

10. We ate one delicious home-cooked dish after another until we were stuffed.[1]

11. We fell asleep as soon as our heads hit the pillows.

12. Almost twenty-four hours had passed since we left home.

B. Write complex sentences.

Step 1 Match a clause from column B with a clause from column A to make a complex sentence.

Step 2 Write the story on the lines provided. The clauses in column A are in the correct order. Be sure to punctuate the sentences correctly.

A	B
1. The trip began badly	a. before we could put on our rain jackets
2. It was almost noon	b. when we had a flat tire on the way to the lake
3. As soon as I threw out my fishing line	c. until I go fishing with my brothers again

---

[1] **stuffed:** very full

4. I spent most of the afternoon untangling[2] my line

5. After we had been fishing for a couple of hours

6. We were totally wet

7. When we got back home

8. It will be a long, long time

d. I immediately took a hot shower

e. while my brothers were catching fish after fish

f. it got caught in some underwater weeds

g. before we started fishing

h. it started to rain

A Miserable Fishing Trip

The trip began badly when we had a flat tire on the way to the lake.

_____

_____

_____

_____

_____

_____

_____

_____

_____

_____

C. Turn back to Practice 5 on page 79. Write complex sentences by combining independent clauses with dependent time clauses as follows.

1. Combine 1 and 2: _____

_____

2. Combine 5 and 6: _____

_____

3. Combine 7 and 8: _____

_____

4. Combine 10 and 11: _____

_____

5. Combine 12 and 13: _____

_____

_____

[2]**untangling:** removing knots, making straight

Sentence Errors: Fragments

In Chapter 2, you learned about the sentence errors called run-ons and comma splices. Another kind of sentence error is called a **fragment**. The word *fragment* means a part of something. A sentence fragment is only part of a sentence or half of a sentence. It is not a complete sentence. These are fragments:

FRAGMENT: Before the test began.

FRAGMENT: As soon as you get home.

Why are they fragments? They are fragments because they are dependent clauses. A dependent clause cannot be a sentence by itself.

To fix this kind of fragment, add an independent clause to it.

COMPLETE SENTENCE: The teacher passed out pencils and paper before the test began.

COMPLETE SENTENCE: Call me as soon as you get home.

PRACTICE 7

Fragments

Identify and correct fragments.

Step 1 Read each sentence. Decide if it is a fragment or a sentence. Write *F* for fragment and *S* for sentence.

Step 2 Then correct each fragment by adding an independent clause. Write your new sentences on the lines provided.

  _F_ 1. Before I learned to speak English well.
  ____ 2. Every night, after I finish my homework.
  ____ 3. As soon as we heard the crash.
  ____ 4. The bicycle racers stopped to rest before they started up the mountain.
  ____ 5. Wait until you hear the bell.
  ____ 6. Whenever my children have a school holiday.
  ____ 7. I work at night while my husband stays home with the children.

1. Before I learned to speak English well, I was afraid to use the telephone.

_____

_____

_____

_____

_____

**Summary:
Three Types
of Sentences**

Let's summarize what you have learned about the three types of sentences. Good writers add interest and variety to their writing by using all three types.

A **simple sentence** has one independent clause.

It was a sunny day.

Raise your hand to ask a question.

A **compound sentence** has two or more independent clauses joined by a comma and a coordinating conjunction.

It was a sunny day, so we went to the beach.

Talk quietly, or don't talk at all.

A **complex sentence** has one independent and one or more dependent clauses. A comma is needed when a dependent clause comes before an independent clause.

While the meat is cooking, prepare the sauce.

Prepare the sauce while the meat is cooking.

PRACTICE 8

*Simple,
Compound,
and Complex
Sentences*

A. Identify the different types of sentences.

Step 1 Underline all independent clauses with a <u>solid line</u> and all dependent clauses with a <u>broken line</u>.

Step 2 In the space at the left, write the words *simple*, *compound*, or *complex* to identify each sentence type.

Unusual Vacations

complex   1. <u>Some people like to relax and do nothing</u> <u>when they take a vacation</u>.

_____   2. Other people like to travel, and still others like to have an adventure.

_____   3. Unusual vacations are becoming popular.

_____   4. For example, people go hiking in Nepal or river rafting in Ecuador.

_____   5. Some people spend their vacations learning, and some spend their vacations helping others.

_____   6. A friend of mine likes to help people, so he spent his summer helping to build a school in Bangladesh.

(continued on next page)

_____ 7. After he returned home, he wanted to go back to help build a medical clinic.

_____ 8. People may find the local scenery a little boring after they have climbed volcanoes in Guatemala or ridden camels in Egypt.

B. The following "how to" paragraph uses a combination of simple, compound, and complex sentences. Find five compound sentences and three complex sentences. Then answer the questions that follow.

How to Succeed in a U.S. College[1]

[1]Succeeding in a U.S. college may require new strategies[2] for students from other cultures. [2]Here are a few tips from a U.S. college professor. [3]First, attend every class. [4]Professors talk about the most important material in class. [5]When you aren't there, you miss important information. [6]Second, take good notes. [7]Then review or recopy your notes as soon as you can. [8]Third, don't be afraid to ask questions whenever you don't understand something. [9]Professors want their students to succeed, so they want them to ask questions. [10]Fourth, get to know your professors personally. [11]Go to their office during office hours, and introduce yourself. [12]Don't waste professors' time, but make sure they know your name and face. [13]Finally, get involved in a campus activity, or get a job in the bookstore. [14]Go to football and basketball games. [15]Join a club. [16]Be friendly, and talk to everyone—other students, professors, secretaries, cafeteria workers, and janitors. [17]Active, involved students are successful students.

1. Which sentences are compound? Sentence numbers ____, ____, ____, ____, and ____.
2. Which sentences are complex? Sentence numbers ____, ____, and ____.

Try It Out! **Step 1** Study the pictures, and discuss the meaning of unfamiliar words.

Step 2 Combine the sentences in each group to make one sentence. Some of your new sentences will be simple, some will be compound, and some will be complex. There may be more than one possible correct way to combine each group.

Step 3 Write the eleven sentences as a paragraph. Add time-order signals to some sentences, but don't start every sentence with a time-order signal.

---

[1]Adapted from Clark Ford, "How To Succeed in College Without falling into the usual traps" [sic], http:www.public.iastate.edu/~cfford101howtosucceed.htm (accessed December 24, 2006).
[2]**strategies:** tactics, approaches

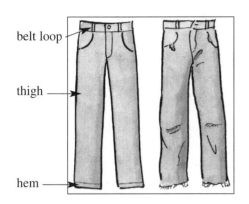

belt loop

thigh

hem

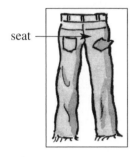

seat

cheese grater

nail file

Word List

Nouns

pair (of jeans)	nail file	hem	sandpaper
denim fabric	thread	spray bottle	thigh
cheese grater	bleach	belt loop	seat

Verbs

afford	spray	dip
rub	fray	bleach

Adjectives

ripped	faded

How to Make Your Own Designer Jeans

1. a. Would you like to own a pair of designer jeans?
   b. You can't afford to pay designer prices.

2. a. Follow these instructions to make your own pair of jeans.
   b. The jeans are stylishly ripped.
   c. The jeans are stylishly faded.

3. a. Buy a pair of inexpensive new jeans.
   b. Use a pair that you already own.

4. a. Find the direction of the lines in the denim fabric.
   b. Rub a knife back and forth in the opposite direction.

5. a. You can also use a cheese grater.
   b. You can also use a nail file.

6. a. Keep rubbing.
   b. White threads appear. (Use *until*.)

spray bottle

7. a. You want the white threads to stay there.
   b. Don't cut them.

8. a. Dip an old toothbrush into bleach.
   b. Run the old toothbrush around the edges of the back pockets.
   c. Run the old toothbrush over the belt loops.

9. a. Mix a little bleach with water in a spray bottle.
   b. Spray the thighs and seat of the jeans.

10. a. Rub sandpaper on the hems of the legs to fray them.
    b. Rip one corner of a back pocket.

11. a. Wash and dry the jeans several times.
    b. Your new jeans will look stylishly old! (Use *after*.)

(continued on next page)

How to Make Your Own Designer Jeans

Would you like to own a pair of designer jeans but can't afford to pay designer prices?

PART 3 | Capitalization and Punctuation

Capitalization: Four More Rules   In Chapter 1, you learned six rules for capitalizing words in English. There are four additional rules in the chart on page 87.

Rules	Examples	
Capitalize:		
7. Names of specific structures such as buildings, roads, and bridges.	the **W**hite **H**ouse the **H**ilton **H**otel the **K**remlin	**H**ighway 395 **S**tate **R**oute 15 the **B**rooklyn **B**ridge
8. Names of specific organizations such as businesses, schools, and clubs.	**S**ears, **R**oebuck & **C**o. **U**nited **N**ations	**C**ity **C**ollege of **N**ew **Y**ork **I**rish **S**tudents' **C**lub
9. Names of the days, months, holidays, and special time periods. BUT NOT the names of seasons.	**M**onday **J**anuary spring summer	**N**ew **Y**ear's **D**ay **R**amadan fall (autumn) winter
10. Geographic areas. BUT NOT compass directions.	the **M**iddle **E**ast the **S**outhwest Drive south for two miles and turn west.	**S**outheast **A**sia **E**astern **E**urope

PRACTICE 9

Capitalization

A. Work with a partner or a group. Write your own examples of Rules 7–10.

Rule 7

a building _____

a road _____

a bridge _____

Rule 8

a business _____

a school or
college _____

a club _____

Rule 9

a day _____

a month _____

a holiday _____

Rule 10

a geographic area
in your country _____

a geographic area
in another part
of the world _____

B. Work by yourself or with a partner. Change the small letters to capital letters wherever necessary in this letter from Heather to her friend Stacie.

A
April 23, 20__

Dear Stacie,

¹I am so happy that you are coming to visit me this summer. ²I hope that you will be able to stay until july 4. ³We are planning a big picnic on that day to celebrate independence day here in the united states.

⁴You asked for directions to my house from the airport, so here they are. ⁵Drive out of the airport and turn north on u.s. 380, then u.s. 680, then california 1. ⁶california 1 is also called nineteenth avenue. ⁷You will pass san francisco state university and a large shopping center.

⁸Continue on nineteenth avenue through golden gate park. ⁹Soon you will come to the famous golden gate bridge. ¹⁰Drive across the bridge and continue north for about ten more miles. ¹¹You will pass the towns of sausalito, mill valley, and larkspur. ¹²In larkspur, take the sir francis drake boulevard exit from the highway.

¹³Drive west for three blocks, and then turn left. ¹⁴Pacific national bank is on the corner where you turn, and across the street is a shell oil company gas station. ¹⁵You will be on elm avenue. ¹⁶Finally, go one block on elm and turn right. ¹⁷My apartment is in the marina towers. ¹⁸The address is 155 west hillside drive.

¹⁹Be sure to bring warm clothes because it is cold in june and july in northern california. ²⁰I can't wait to see you!

Love,

Heather

Commas: Four Rules

There are many rules for using commas. You have already learned three of them:

Rules	Examples
Use a comma:	
1. After listing-order and time-order signals (EXCEPT *then*).	First, put four cups of rice into a pan. After that, fold the paper in half again. After the test, go out and celebrate.
2. Before coordinating conjunctions in a compound sentence. *Exception*: Sometimes writers omit this comma in very short sentences.	Some people like to travel, and others like to have an adventure. Cook the steak over high heat for six minutes, but don't let it burn. Dogs bark and cats meow. Turn left and drive one block
3. In a complex sentence when a dependent adverb clause comes before an independent clause.	While you are waiting for the pizza dough to rise, make the sauce. After you take the pizza out of the oven, cut it into eight pieces.

Here is a fourth comma rule.

Use a comma:	
4. To separate items in a series. A series is three or more things. These may be words or phrases (groups of words).	One dog, one cat, two goldfish, a bird, and four humans live at our house. Every morning I get up early, run a mile, take a shower, eat breakfast, and feed my pets. Turn left at the stoplight, go one block, and turn right.

Notice that there is always one less comma than items. If there are four items, there are three commas; if there are five items, there are four commas; and so on.

> ### Writer's Tips
>
> 1. If there are three items in a series, some writers omit the last comma. However, it is a good idea to use all the commas because commas make your meaning clearer.
>
>   I have visited many countries in Europe, Asia, and America.
>
>   Shopping, relaxing, and visiting friends are my favorite weekend activities.
>
> 2. With only two items, don't use any commas.
>
>   I have visited many countries in Europe and Asia.
>
>   Sleeping and hanging out with friends are my teenage son's favorite weekend activities.

PRACTICE 10

Commas

A. Add commas where necessary in the following paragraphs. Add twenty commas to Paragraph 1 and eight commas to Paragraph 2.

Paragraph 1

My Brother, the Sports Fan

[1]My brother Bob is a sports fan. [2]His favorite sports are golf tennis skiing and swimming. [3]He skis in the winter swims in the summer and plays golf during the spring summer and fall. [4]He also watches football and baseball on TV. [5]His bedroom looks like a used sporting goods store. [6]Bob owns skis tennis racquets golf clubs footballs basketballs baseballs tennis balls soccer balls a bicycle and weights. [7]Whenever he comes home from a sports event he throws his equipment in a pile on his bed. [8]When the pile gets too high you can't see his bed his desk or sometimes even him.

Paragraph 2

How to Fail a Driving Test

[1]It's easy to fail a driving test if you really try. [2]First park your car so close to the next car that the examiner cannot get into your car to begin the test. [3]It also helps to have your two front wheels far up on the curb—blocking the sidewalk if possible. [4]Second back out of the parking space really fast. [5]After that try to hit something such as another car. [6]Don't stop at stop signs but speed up to get through intersections quickly. [7]Then try to make your tires squeal while turning corners. [8]Next look for an opportunity to turn the wrong way on a one-way street. [9]Entering a one-way street in the wrong direction will cause you to fail immediately. [10]Finally don't stop for pedestrians in crosswalks but use your horn to frighten them out of your way. [11]Just one of these techniques will probably get you an F on a driving test and two or more certainly will.

B. Complete these sentences to practice the "items in a series" comma rule.

1. What three foods do you like the most? (*Use* and *before the last item.*)
   I like __Japanese sushi, Middle Eastern falafel, and Mexican tacos__ .

2. What three foods don't you like? (*Use* or *before the last item.*)
   I don't like _____.

3. What are three places you might go on your honeymoon. (*Use* or *before the last item.*)
   On my honeymoon, I might go to _____

   _____.

4. What are six useful items to take on a hike? (*Use* and *before the last item.*)
   Whenever you go on a hike, be sure to take _____

   _____.

5. What are two animals that don't get along with each other. (*Use* and.)
   _____ don't get along with each other.

(continued on next page)

6. What are three things you do every morning? (*Use* and.)
   Every morning, I _____

   _____.

7. What are two things you always do and one thing you never do on weekends. (*Use both* and *and* but. *Write a compound sentence.*)
   On weekends, I always _____

   _____.

Try It Out!   Write a paragraph giving directions from one place to another place in your city, in your neighborhood, or on the campus of your school.

- Practice using capitalization rules by giving the names of streets, buildings, stores, and other landmarks.
- Practice writing complex sentences. Try to include at least three complex sentences in your paragraph.

For fun, read your paragraph to a classmate. See if he or she can draw a map showing your directions.

PART 4 | Writing

Review Questions   Check your understanding of the important points in this chapter by answering the following questions.

Organization

1. What are the four keys to writing clear instructions?
2. What two orders can you use to organize a "how to" paragraph?
3. What are some time-order signals?

Sentence Structure

4. What is an independent clause?
5. What is a dependent clause?
6. What is a complex sentence, and how do you punctuate one?
7. What is a fragment?
8. How do you correct a fragment?

Capitalization and Punctuation

9. What are the four capitalization rules in this chapter?
10. What are four comma rules that you have learned in Chapters 1–3?

Writing Assignment

Choose one of the topics from Practice 1A or 1B on pages 69–70, and write a paragraph giving instructions. Use time order or listing order to organize the steps.

Step 1 Prewrite to get ideas.

- Use the listing technique.
- Edit your list.
- Put the steps in order (time order or listing order).
- Make an outline.

Step 2 Write the first draft.

- Write ROUGH DRAFT at the top of your paper.
- Begin with a topic sentence that names the topic and indicates that you will give instructions.
- Follow your outline.
- Add time-order or listing-order signals to some of the steps.
- Try to include at least three complex sentences in your paragraph.

Step 3 Edit the first draft.

- Edit your paragraph with a partner as you have done in previous chapters. Use the Reader's Response 3B and Writer's Self-Check 3B on pages 200 and 201.

Step 4 Write the final copy.

Write a neat final copy of your paragraph to hand in to your teacher. Your teacher may also ask you to hand in your prewriting, your outline, and your other drafts.

Describing a Place

Chapter Preview

Chapter Preview

In this chapter, you will write paragraphs in which you describe places. You will also study and practice:

- space order
- descriptive details
- the order of adjectives
- prepositional phrases
- varying sentence openings

Prewriting Activity: Listing Descriptive Details

Descriptions are "word pictures." You tell how something looks, feels, smells, tastes, and sounds. You need to become a sharp observer and notice many small details so that you can write a good word picture.

1. Discuss each picture on the next pages with your partner or group. What kind of person do you think lives or works in each place?

2. What clues in each picture led you to your choice? Make a list of the clues next to each picture. Use the word list on page 96 for picture 1.

1. **Picture 1 Clues**

_____

_____

_____

_____

_____

_____

_____

_____

_____

Name of room: _____

Kind of person: _____

_____

(continued on next page)

Word List for Picture 1

Nouns

bed	dresser	headset	poster
bedspread	electric guitar	lamp	sheet
closet	electronic equipment	mattress	speaker
dresser drawer	electronics	pillow	sports shoes

Adjectives

cluttered	disorganized	messy	open

2. **Picture 2 Clues**

_____

_____

_____

_____

_____

_____

_____

_____

_____

Name of room: _____

Kind of person: _____

_____

Word List for Picture 2

Nouns

bookshelves	framed award	leather chair	rug
drapes	framed certificate	oil painting	swivel chair
executive desk	guest chair	picture window	

Adjectives

expensive	formal	impressive	luxurious

3. **Picture 3 Clues**

_____
_____
_____
_____
_____
_____
_____
_____

Name of room: _____
Kind of person: _____

_____

Word List for Picture 3

Nouns

chrome	helmet	motorcycle	screwdriver
engine part	jacket	pliers	tool
engine	leather	rag	wrench
exhaust pipes			

Adjectives

chrome	greasy	messy	oily
disorganized	leather	neat	organized

Keep your lists. You will use one of them later to write a paragraph.

PART 1 | Organization

Description   In this chapter, you will learn to write a good description. When you write a description, you tell what something—a person, an object, or a place—looks like.

> There are two keys to writing good descriptions:
>
> 1. Use space order to organize your description.
> 2. Use lots of descriptive details.

Space Order   Imagine that you are standing in the doorway of your classroom. How would you describe the room to someone who has never seen it? Here are some possibilities:

- You might start at the left side of the doorway and work your way around the room in a clockwise direction to the right side, ending at the doorway again.

- You might start at the front of the room and go from front to back, first describing the chalkboard, the teacher's desk, and the area around the teacher's desk. Then you might describe the students' desks in the center of the room, and finally the walls and/or windows at the back and sides of the room.

This kind of organization is called **space order**. Here are other kinds of space order that you can use to write a description:

top to bottom	bottom to top	right to left	left to right
far to near	near to far	outside to inside	inside to outside

The refrigerator in the picture is described in the model paragraph on the next page. As you read the model, look for phrases that tell you the location of things.

MODEL

Space Order

The Shared Refrigerator

¹My roommate and I share a refrigerator. ²My roommate's half of our refrigerator is very neat. ³On the top shelf is a carton of milk, a pitcher of orange juice, and a bottle of mineral water. ⁴These are arranged in a straight line on the shelf. ⁵On the next shelf are cans of soda. ⁶These are carefully lined up in rows. ⁷Orange soda is in the first row, cola in the second, and lemon lime in the third. ⁸On the third shelf, he keeps dairy foods, such as butter, cheese, eggs, and yogurt. ⁹On the bottom shelf sit plastic containers of leftovers.¹ ¹⁰These are neatly arranged by size. ¹¹The large ones are in the back, and the small ones are in the front. ¹²There are two drawers in the bottom of the refrigerator. ¹³In his drawer, my roommate keeps vegetables and fruit. ¹⁴Each item is in a separate plastic bag in the drawer. ¹⁵In conclusion, my roommate is an organized person, and his half of our refrigerator really reflects his personality.

Questions on the Model

1. Which sentence is the topic sentence? (*Hint*: It is not in its usual location.)
2. Which space order did the writer use? Choose from the list on the preceding page.

Topic and Concluding Sentences for Descriptive Paragraphs

The topic part of a topic sentence for a paragraph of description usually names the person, place, or thing to be described. The controlling idea part usually gives a general impression (*beautiful, neat, messy, interesting, unusual, crowded, busy, noisy,* and so on. Here are some examples of topic sentences for paragraphs of description.

```
      ┌──── TOPIC ────┐┌──── CONTROLLING IDEA ────┐
      The old house looked ready to fall down.
```

```
      ┌── TOPIC ──┐┌──────── CONTROLLING IDEA ────────┐
      The cave was a dangerous place to enter.
```

```
      ┌─ TOPIC ─┐┌──────── CONTROLLING IDEA ────────┐
      The club was full of young people having fun.
```

---

¹**leftovers:** food that was not eaten at an earlier meal

The concluding sentence of a description may repeat the idea stated in the topic sentence. In the model paragraph, the writer used different words to repeat the idea that the roommate's side of the refrigerator is neat. It may also give the writer's opinion or feeling about the topic. Here are other examples of concluding sentences for paragraphs of description.

> In short, I doubt the old house will survive one more winter.

> My friend and I were very happy when we got out of the cave.

> To sum up, music, dancing, and flashing lights make clubs exciting and fun.

PRACTICE 1

Space Order

Read the following description of a person. Then answer the questions about the organization of the paragraph that follow.

My Tall Nephew

[1]The first thing you notice about my nephew is that he is extremely tall—six feet, six inches tall, to be exact. [2]His head sticks up almost a foot above everyone else's. [3]His hair is short, light brown, and curly, and his eyes are blue. [4]His nose is straight, and his mouth curls into a smile easily and often. [5]His casual clothes are typical of young people everywhere: a T-shirt and jeans. [6]On the front of his shirt, you can read the name of his school in red and blue letters. [7]As your eyes move down his long legs, you notice that his jeans are a little too short. [8]Perhaps he can't buy pants to fit his long legs and narrow waist, or perhaps he doesn't care much about clothes. [9]On his feet, he wears sneakers. [10]Maybe his sneakers were white when they were new, but now they are gray with age and wear. [11]Despite his casual clothes,[1] my nephew is not a casual person. [12]He stands as tall and straight as a redwood[2] tree, and you think to yourself, "This is a strong and confident young man."

1. Analyze the topic sentence. Circle the topic and underline the controlling idea.

2. What is the nephew's most noticeable physical feature?

   _____

3. Which sentence is the concluding sentence? What word in the topic sentence is repeated in the concluding sentence?

   _____

4. What kind of space order does the writer of this paragraph use? Choose from the list on page 98.

   _____

---

[1]**despite his casual clothes:** The meaning is, "He wears casual clothes, but he is not a casual person."
[2]**redwood:** a kind of tree that grows very tall and straight

Specific Details

The second key to writing a good description is to use specific details. When you describe something, you paint a picture with words. Your goal is to make your reader "see" what you have described. The way to do this is to use a lot of specific details. Specific means exact or precise. The opposite of specific is too general, or vague. The more specific you can be, the better your reader can see what you are describing.

Here are some examples:

Vague	Specific
a lot of money	$500,000
a large house	a six-bedroom, four-bathroom house
a nice car	a Lexus
jogs a lot	jogs three miles in the park every day
a pretty face	warm brown eyes, shining black hair, and sparkling white teeth

PRACTICE 2

Being Specific

Work with a partner. Add as many specific details as you can to these vague descriptions. Use present tense verbs in your sentences. Then compare your details with those of other students.

1. My uncle is large.
   a. <u>He is six feet, three inches tall and weighs 250 pounds.</u>
   b. <u>He wears size fifteen shoes.</u>
   c. <u>His shirts are XXX Large.</u>
   d. <u>He can hold a basketball upside-down in one hand.</u>

2. My boss has a nice house.
   a. _____
   b. _____
   c. _____
   d. _____

3. Carl is a bad driver.
   a. _____
   b. _____
   c. _____
   d. _____

(continued on next page)

4. The inside of the taxicab was dirty.

    a. _____

    b. _____

    c. _____

    d. _____

5. The student cafeteria was noisy and crowded.

    a. _____

    b. _____

    c. _____

    d. _____

PRACTICE 3

Adding Specific Details

Work with a group.

Step 1 Choose one person to be the secretary.

Step 2 Rewrite the paragraph to make the details more specific. Don't change the first sentence. Rewrite the other sentences, and write at least ten new sentences to add specific details.

Step 3 Compare your paragraph with other groups' paragraphs. Which space order did each group use?

The Limousine

The limousine was quite luxurious. It was big. The outside was nice. The inside was nice. It had nice seats. It had an entertainment center. It also had food and beverages. Our ride was fun.

The Limousine

     The limousine was quite luxurious. It was at least fifteen feet long. It had six doors and could carry ten passengers comfortably. The outside of the limousine . . .

_____

_____

_____

_____

_____

_____

_____

_____

_____

_____

Planning a Space-Order Paragraph

You plan a space-order paragraph the same way you plan a time-order paragraph. First, decide which space order to use—right to left, left to right, front to back, and so on. Then list your details in that order. Finally, make an outline by adding a topic sentence, capital letters to each detail, and a concluding sentence.

PRACTICE 4

Space-Order Outline

Here is a partly completed outline of the model paragraph on page 99, "The Shared Refrigerator." Complete the outline by filling in the missing main details. Use the top-to-bottom organization of the paragraph to help you select them.

The Shared Refrigerator

My roommate's half of our refrigerator is very neat.

    A. On the top shelf is a carton of milk, a pitcher of orange juice, and a bottle of mineral water.

    B. On the next shelf _____

    C. _____

    D. _____

    E. _____

My roommate is an organized person, and his half of our refrigerator really reflects his personality.

Try It Out! Make an outline for a paragraph describing one of the pictures in the Prewriting Activity at the beginning of the chapter. Your outline should look like the one in Practice 4 on page 103. Do not write the paragraph yet. You will do that later.

Step 1 Write a topic sentence that names the place and tells what kind of person lives or works there. For example, your first sentence for the picture of the office might be one of these:

> This is the office of a very important person.
>
> An important business executive works in this office.

Step 2 List the main details that describe the room. List them in space order, and give each detail a capital letter (A, B, C, and so on).

Step 3 Write a concluding sentence that tells your feeling or opinion about the place. For example, you could write:

> I hope to work in an office like this one some day.

Step 4 Remember to give your outline a title.

PART 2 | Grammar

In this section, you will learn how to use adjectives to make a description vivid and interesting.

Adjectives Adjectives describe nouns and pronouns. Adjectives tell what things (or people) look like, what kind they are, or how many of them there are. Adjectives answer the questions: *What kind? Which one?* and *How many?*

what kind?	the **old** car with the **broken** window
which one?	the **fourth** chapter of the book, **his** car
how many?	**twelve** students, a **few** students

Here are some things to know about adjectives.

1. Adjectives always come in front of nouns, not after them.

   twelve talented young musicians

2. Adjectives can also follow linking verbs.

be	The children are **happy**.
seem	You seem **sad**.
look	Brides always look **beautiful**.
smell	The cookies smell **delicious**.
taste	Candy tastes **sweet**.
feel	Silk feels **smooth**.

3. English has a kind of adjective called a compound adjective. A compound adjective is two or more words that function together as one word. A compound adjective often has a hyphen or hyphens between its parts.

   ten-week semester   **part-time** job   **two-year-old** child

4. Adjectives are always singular. Never add *s* to an adjective, and never use a plural word as an adjective.

big feet	(not bigs feet)
terrible memories	(not terribles memories)

   Be especially careful when a compound adjective containing a number comes before a noun.

a **six-foot** wall	(not a six-feet wall)
a **five-dollar** bill	(not a five-dollars bill)
a **two-year-old** child	(not a two-years-old child)

   Of course, when words such as *foot, dollar,* and *year* are nouns, they can be plural.

   The wall is six **feet** high.

   The book costs five **dollars**.

   The child is two **years** old.

5. Nouns can be adjectives.

the **English** book	a **shoe** store
some **tennis** balls	the **Japanese** students

6. Proper adjectives (adjectives referring to nationalities, languages, geographic places, and so on) are capitalized.

Egyptian custom	**Cuban** government
Spanish class	**Asian** languages

7. *-ing* and *-ed* words can be adjectives.

swimming pool	**bored** students
cooking class	**used** car
sleeping baby	**broken** heart
boring class	**stolen** money

PRACTICE 5

*Identifying
Adjectives*

1. Circle all the adjectives in the following paragraph. (Some sentences may not have any.)

2. Which space order did the writer of this paragraph use?

_____

_____

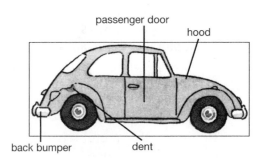

My First Car

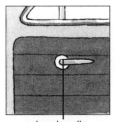

door handle

¹My first car was old and ugly but I loved it anyway. ²Its main paint color was black, but it also had blue, green, yellow, and white paint in different places. ³The body was in terrible condition. ⁴It had several big dents. ⁵The lock on the hood was broken, so I had to tie it down with a strong rope. ⁶Also, the back bumper was rusty, and the front window was cracked. ⁷The inside of the car was also in terrible condition. ⁸The passenger door handle was missing, so you couldn't open the passenger door from the inside. ⁹The seats had at least ten large holes in them. ¹⁰Also, the gas gauge was broken. ¹¹It always showed "full," so I often ran out of gas. ¹²The speedometer was broken too, so I never knew how fast I was driving. ¹³Like a first love, my old VW had a few faults,¹ but in my mind it was perfect.

gas gauge

speedometer

_____

¹**faults:** flaws; problems; bad or nonworking parts

Order of Adjectives

When you write several adjectives in a row, sometimes you must put them in a particular order, and sometimes you can choose your own order depending on the kind of adjective. One kind is called **cumulative adjectives**, and the other kind is called **coordinate adjectives**.

Cumulative Adjectives	Coordinate Adjectives
The **poor little black** dog	The **wet, cold,** (and) **hungry** dog
	The **cold, wet,** (and) **hungry** dog
	The **hungry, wet,** (and) **cold** dog

Cumulative Adjectives

Cumulative adjectives always go before a noun. They must be in a particular order. For example, you cannot write *the little black poor dog*; you **must** write *the poor little black dog*. Do not put commas between cumulative adjectives.

The following list shows you the order of cumulative adjectives.

Order of Cumulative Adjectives[2]		
Kind of Adjective	**Examples**	
1. Articles, demonstrative pronouns, possessives	an, an, the, this, that, these, those, her, their, Mary's	
2. Quantity	two, fifty, some, many, (a) few	
3. Opinion	poor, beautiful, interesting, cheerful, expensive	
4. Appearance	*Size*	big, little
	Shape/Length	round, square, short, long
	Condition	rusty, broken, hungry, wet, cold
5. Age, color	old, new, young black, red, blond	
6. Nationality, religion	Guatemalan, European, Congolese, Asian Catholic, Muslim, Buddhist, Jewish, Protestant	
7. Material, purpose	silk, wood, cotton, gold, metal swimming, reading, hiking	
8. Noun used as an adjective	shoe (as in *shoe store*), wedding (as in *wedding dress*)	

---

[2]Students may encounter exceptions to the order of adjectives presented here.

Writer's Tip

It is possible to use several cumulative adjectives in a row, but using too many adjectives confuses your reader and weakens your description. In general, do not use more than three cumulative adjectives in a row.

The bride wore **her mother's beautiful satin wedding** dress.

PRACTICE 6

Cumulative Adjectives

Add the cumulative adjectives in parentheses to describe the underlined noun in each sentence. Add them in the correct order and write the sentences on the lines provided.

1. There were <u>toys</u> in the middle of the floor. (broken, several, plastic)
   There were several broken plastic toys in the middle of the floor.

2. <u>Clouds</u> announced an approaching rainstorm. (black, big)

3. <u>Flags</u> hung from every window. (colorful, rectangular)

4. Children played on the <u>grass</u>. (green, thick)

5. I dream about relaxing on a <u>beach</u>. (sand, white, beautiful)

6. They got married in a <u>church</u>. (stone, small, Italian)

7. The parents left <u>children</u> with the grandparents while they worked. (young, their, two)

_____

_____

8. <u>Class</u> has thirty students. (advanced, Mr. Thompson's, English)

_____

_____

9. The real estate agent pointed out <u>problems</u> with the house. (minor, several)

_____

_____

10. <u>Windows</u> were broken. (large, bedroom, four)

_____

_____

Coordinate Adjectives

Coordinate adjectives can go before a noun or after a linking verb. You can write coordinate adjectives in any order, and you separate them from each other with commas. Also,

- When coordinate adjectives come before a noun, you may put the word _and_ before the last one (but you don't have to).
- When two or more coordinate adjectives come after a linking verb, you **must** put _and_ before the last one.

Before a noun (_and_ optional)	A **hungry, cold, wet** dog sat outside our front door. A **wet, cold**, <u>and</u> **hungry** dog sat outside our front door.
After a linking verb (_and_ required)	The dog was **hungry, wet**, <u>and</u> **cold**.

PRACTICE 7

Coordinate Adjectives

Add commas to the coordinate adjectives in the following sentences.

1. The people want a smart, experienced, honest leader.
2. Most students like friendly enthusiastic imaginative teachers.
3. I am tired of the cold rainy weather.
4. I am looking forward to the warm sunny relaxing days of summer.
5. The prince in a fairy tale is either tall dark and handsome or tall blond and handsome.
6. A fairy-tale prince is never short bald and ugly.

PRACTICE 8

Cumulative and Coordinate Adjectives

Step 1 Underline each adjective in the following sentences.

Step 2 Mark each one *cum.* for cumulative or *coord.* for coordinate.

Step 3 Add commas where they are necessary.

           cum.   coord. coord.

1. I found a <u>small</u> piece of <u>smelly</u>, <u>moldy</u>[1] cheese under my bed.

2. Four shiny black limousines were parked outside the hotel.

3. The small red apples looked sweet crisp juicy and delicious.

4. Hundreds of happy cheering football fans ran onto the field.

5. The pretty new French teacher is from Quebec.

6. My father bought a beautiful antique Persian rug as a twentieth anniversary gift for my mother.

PRACTICE 9

Editing Adjectives

Find and correct the errors in the following sentences. In some sentences, commas are missing. In other sentences, adjectives are in the wrong order.

1. The hungry frightened dog waited for someone to feed him.

2. The black little dog waited for someone to feed him.

3. My mother always bakes a chocolate delicious cake for my little brother's birthday.

4. For his tenth birthday, he received a metal new baseball bat.

5. The coach's enthusiastic supportive manner gave the team confidence.

---

[1]**moldy:** covered with a soft green or black substance, like old bread

PRACTICE 10

Writing Sentences with Adjectives

Write sentences describing objects you might find under the bed of a "pack rat."[2] Use at least two adjectives (either cumulative or coordinate) to describe each object. Use your imagination!

1. Under the bed, I saw <u> several fuzzy dust balls   </u>.

2. I also saw a pair of _____.

3. Then I discovered a box of _____.

4. Next to it, I found a greasy paper bag with _____

_____ inside it.

5. The discovery of _____

_____ didn't surprise me.

Try It Out! Write a paragraph from the outline you made describing a room for the Try It Out! on page 104. Complete the steps in the writing process. (You have already completed Step 1, Prewriting.)

Step 2 Write the first draft.

- Write ROUGH DRAFT at the top of your paper.
- Follow your outline, which is in space order.
- Make your description vivid and interesting by adding adjectives to the details. For example, instead of writing "There is a pen and pencil set on the desk," add adjectives, such as *shiny, silver, expensive*, and so on.

  There is a shiny silver pen and pencil set on the desk.

Step 3 Edit the first draft.

- Edit your paragraph with a partner as you have done in previous chapters. Use the Reader's Response 4A and Writer's Self-Check 4A on pages 202 and 203.

Step 4 Write the final copy.

- Write a neat final copy of your paragraph to hand in to your teacher. Your teacher may also ask you to hand in your prewriting, your outline, and your other drafts.

---

[2]**pack rat:** a person who never throws anything away (slang)

PART 3 | Sentence Structure

Prepositions **Prepositions** are little words such as *of, to, from, in*, and *at*. Most prepositions are one word. A few prepositions are two words (*because of*) or three words (*in front of*). Here is a list of common prepositions.

about	besides	near	under
above	between	of	until
across	beyond	off	upon
after	by	on	with
against	down	out	without
along	during	outside	according to
around	except	over	because of
at	for	since	in addition to
before	from	through	in back of
behind	in	throughout	in front of
below	inside	till	in place of
beneath	into	to	next to
beside	like	toward	out of

Writer's Tip

Some words, such as *to*, are sometimes prepositions and sometimes another part of speech. Compare these two sentences.

1. We went to the supermarket.
2. We wanted to buy some fruit.

In sentence 1, *to* is a preposition because it is followed by a noun (*the supermarket*). In sentence 2, the word *to* is part of the infinitive verb phrase *to buy*.

Prepositional Phrases

A preposition is usually combined with a noun or noun phrase to make a **prepositional phrase**, such as *in the house* or *at six o'clock*.

Some prepositional phrases answer the question *where*. These are prepositional phrases of place. Prepositional phrases of place are useful in space-order paragraphs to show the location of objects in a description.

on the desk	opposite the door
next to the window	in the closet
under the bed	in the middle of the room
in front of the house	in the distance

Other prepositional phrases answer the question *when*. These are prepositional phrases of time. Prepositional phrases of time are useful in "how to" paragraphs to give the order of the steps.

at last	before the test
after that	upon arrival
after class	in the morning
on New Year's Day	at midnight

Other prepositional phrases show possession:

(the father) of the bride	(the colors) of the rainbow
(the name) of my boss	(the president) of the company

Others describe or identify someone or something:

(the woman) with red hair	(the man) in the blue shirt
(the student) from Ecuador	(the car) with the flat tire

As you read the model paragraph, look for prepositional phrases. Put parentheses around them.

MODEL

Prepositional Phrases of Place in a Description

My Desk

¹The inside (of my desk) looks (like a second-hand store.) ²Each drawer is full of junk. ³In the center drawer, you can find paper clips, erasers, pencils, pens, rubber bands, and small bottles of glue. ⁴I have a small hardware store in my top drawer. ⁵If you want to repair something, you can find whatever you need there. ⁶In the second drawer, I keep snacks in case I get hungry at night. ⁷Small items of clothing are in the third drawer, and the bottom drawer holds my collection of wind-up toys. ⁸I play with them during study breaks. ⁹I have such a variety of things in my desk that I could start a small business, according to my friends.

Questions on the Model

1. Which space order did the writer of this paragraph use?
2. How many prepositional phrases are there in the model?
3. How many of them tell where something is?

Using Prepositional Phrases to Vary Sentence Openings

One way to improve your writing is to start sentences with prepositional phrases of time and place. A paragraph in which every sentence follows the same subject–verb–object pattern can be boring. Vary your sentence openings by sometimes starting a sentence with a prepositional phrase. Notice that you put a comma after a prepositional phrase at the beginning of a sentence.

USUAL PATTERN:	Get eight hours of sleep before a big exam.
NEW PATTERN:	Before a big exam, get eight hours of sleep.
USUAL PATTERN:	I keep snacks in the second drawer.
NEW PATTERN:	In the second drawer, I keep snacks.

Moving a prepositional phrase is also possible in sentences beginning with *there is/there are* and *there was/there were*.

USUAL PATTERN:	There is a secret hiding place under the stairs.
NEW PATTERN:	Under the stairs, there is a secret hiding place.
USUAL PATTERN:	There are several kinds of trees in the park.
NEW PATTERN:	In the park, there are several kinds of trees.

Sometimes the subject of a sentence can just exchange places with a prepositional phrase of place. This can happen when the sentence contains only a subject, an intransitive verb (a verb that has no object), and a prepositional phrase. In this case, don't use a comma.

USUAL PATTERN: A comfortable chair is in the corner.
[—— S ——] V [— PP —]

NEW PATTERN: In the corner is a comfortable chair.

USUAL PATTERN: A picture of Beethoven hangs above her piano.
[—— S ——] V [— PP —]

NEW PATTERN: Above her piano hangs a picture of Beethoven.

PRACTICE 11

Prepositional Phrases

A. Identify and punctuate prepositional phrases of time and place.

Step 1 Put parentheses around all prepositional phrases.

Step 2 Add a comma after prepositional phrases of time and place that begin a sentence.

My Favorite Place

¹My favorite place (on the campus) (of our school) is the lawn (in front of the library.) ²(During my lunch break,) I go there to relax (with friends.) ³In the center of the lawn there is a fountain. ⁴Water splashes from the fountain onto some rocks around it. ⁵The sound of the splashing water reminds me of a place in the mountains where we go in the summer. ⁶Under a group of trees at the edge of the lawn are wooden benches and tables. ⁷On warm days students sit at the tables in the shade of the trees to eat their lunches. ⁸The chatter¹ of students makes studying impossible. ⁹After lunch it becomes quiet again.

B. Improve the paragraph on the next page by moving some of the prepositional phrases of time and place to the beginning of their sentences.

Step 1 Put parentheses around prepositional phrases of time and place.

Step 2 Then rewrite the paragraph on the lines provided. Move two or three prepositional phrases of time and place to the beginning of their sentences. Do not change every sentence.

---

¹**chatter:** noisy talking

My Childhood Hideout[1]

[1]I had a secret hiding place (near my childhood home.) [2]No one knew of its existence, so it became my refuge[2] from the world. [3]I often went there to escape from my older brothers and sisters. [4]I would sit alone for hours and daydream. [5]I was quite comfortable in my hideout. [6]An old rug covered the floor. [7]A pillow and blanket that I had permanently "borrowed" from my oldest (and meanest) brother were along one wall. [8]A metal box with a strong lid was in the corner. [9]The box contained snacks, a flashlight, and a few of my favorite mystery novels. [10]I could spend all day in my hideout.

My Childhood Hideout

_____

_____

_____

_____

_____

_____

_____

_____

_____

_____

_____

_____

_____

_____

---

[1]**hideout:** hiding place
[2]**refuge:** place of safety

Try It Out! **Step 1** Combine the sentences in each group to make one sentence. There may be more than one possible correct way to combine each group.

Step 2 Write the sentences as a paragraph on page 118. Put prepositional phrases at the beginning of some sentences to show the space order.

The Shared Refrigerator (*continued*)

1. a. My half of our refrigerator is messy.
   b. My half of our refrigerator is disorganized.

2. a. A box of eggs sits on the shelf.
   b. The eggs are broken.
   c. The shelf is the top one.

3. a. Carrots and salami share the shelf.
   b. The shelf is the second one.
   c. They share it with bread and lettuce.
   d. The carrots are old.
   e. The salami is brown.
   f. The bread is hard.
   g. The bread is green.
   h. The lettuce is soft.

4. a. Pizza lies under a bowl of spaghetti.
   b. The pizza is leftover.
   c. The spaghetti is three weeks old.
   d. These things lie on the third shelf.

5. a. The bottom drawer holds a combination.
   b. The combination is interesting.
   c. The combination is of paper bags of food.
   d. The food is from McDonald's.
   e. The food is from Taco Bell.
   f. The food is from the Chinese Kitchen.

6. a. A puddle covers the bottom.
   b. The puddle is smelly.
   c. The puddle is disgusting.

7. a. My roommate and I are different.
   b. We get along.
   c. We do this very well.

(continued on next page)

The Shared Refrigerator (*continued*)

My half of our refrigerator is messy and disorganized.

_____

_____

_____

_____

_____

_____

_____

_____

_____

_____

_____

_____

_____

PART 4 | Writing

Review Questions

Check your understanding of the important points in this chapter by answering the following questions.

Organization

1. What are the two keys to a good description?
2. What are some different kinds of space order?
3. How can you help your reader "see" what you have described?

Grammar

4. What does an adjective do?
5. Where are two places in a sentence that you can find adjectives?
6. What is special about cumulative adjectives? Do you put commas between cumulative adjectives?
7. How are coordinate adjectives different from cumulative ones? Do you put commas between coordinate adjectives?

Sentence Structure

8. What is a prepositional phrase?
9. What are two types of prepositional phrases and what do they do?
10. How can you use prepositional phrases to improve your writing?

Writing Assignment

Write a paragraph in which you describe a place that is special to you, or choose one of these topic suggestions.

Topic Suggestions

Your classroom

The student cafeteria at lunchtime

Your grandmother's kitchen

A crowded bus on a hot day

The subway at rush hour

A club on a weekend night

A beach at sunset

A holiday parade

Your bedroom or room where you study

Your favorite room in your house

Your neighborhood

A hospital emergency room

The town square on market day

The apartment or home of a pack rat

Your dream house

The clothes closet of a *fashionista*[1]

---

[1]*fashionista:* person interested in clothing and fashion

Follow the steps in the writing process.

Step 1 Prewrite to get ideas.

- Use the prewriting technique that is most productive for you: freewriting, clustering, or listing.
- Make an outline.

Step 2 Write the first draft.

- Write ROUGH DRAFT at the top of your paper.
- Begin your paragraph with a topic sentence that names the place and gives a main idea about it. You can give its general size or condition or a general impression. Use an adjective, such as *big, small, luxurious, messy, beautiful, plain, wild, mysterious*, or *comfortable*.
- Use space order (right to left, top to bottom, far to near, and so on) to organize your sentences. Use prepositional phrases to show the order. Put some of the prepositional phrases at the beginning of their sentences.
- Write several sentences that give descriptive details. You can describe objects, and you can also tell what people are doing in the place. Use adjectives in your descriptive details.
- End your paragraph with a sentence that tells your feeling about the place.

Step 3 Edit the first draft.

- Edit your paragraph with a partner as you have done in previous chapters. Use the Reader's Response 4B and Writer's Self-Check 4B on pages 204 and 205.

Step 4 Write the final copy.

- Write a neat final copy of your paragraph to hand in to your teacher. Your teacher may also ask you to hand in your prewriting, your outline, and your other drafts.

Stating Reasons and Using Examples

Chapter Preview

In this unit, you will write another listing-order paragraph using reasons and examples to prove your points. You will also study and practice:

- outlines with details
- transition signals with reasons
- transition signals with examples
- two more capitalization rules
- four more comma rules

Prewriting Activity: Reasons and Examples

1. A friend from home has asked you to recommend a language school. You, of course, want your friend to come to your school. With a partner or a small group, discuss various reasons your friend should come to your school.

Here are some points to consider.

classes	cost	campus facilities (gymnasium, computer lab, dormitories, etc.)
teachers	location	
other students	nearby attractions	student success rate

2. Use the space below to take notes or to use the freewriting, clustering, or listing techniques to get ideas. Try to find at least four reasons.

Reasons to Study at _____

3. Now do more thinking to find one or two specific examples for each reason. A specific example might be the name of a class (TOEFL Preparation), a favorite teacher (Mrs. Oser), a campus facility (the computer lab), or a school activity (Welcome Week). A specific example could also be a cost ($600 per semester) or a distance (20 miles to the nearest surfing beach).

4. Complete the outline.

Outline

_____ is a good place to learn English

       (name of school)

for several reasons.

Reason A: _____

    Example: _____

    Example: _____

Reason B: _____

    Example: _____

    Example: _____

Reason C: _____

    Example: _____

    Example: _____

Reason D: _____

    Example: _____

    Example: _____

PART 1 | Organization

In this section, you will learn to write about reasons and use examples to support your reasons. Read the model paragraph below. Then answer the questions.

MODEL

Reasons and Examples

Costa Rica

¹Costa Rica is a great place to spend a vacation for two reasons. ²First of all, Costa Rica has an excellent system of national parks where visitors can observe nature. ³For example, in Tortuguero National Park, visitors can watch sea turtles come ashore¹ to lay their eggs in nests in the sand. ⁴Then they can come back several months later to see the new babies crawl down to the sea. ⁵In Santa Rosa National Park, visitors can see unusual birds, such as toucans and quetzals. ⁶They can also observe exotic animals, such as spider monkeys. ⁷Second, Costa Rica has many beautiful beaches. ⁸For instance, the beaches at Manuel Antonio National Park are among the most beautiful in the world, and the beaches on Cañoa and Cocos Islands offer perfect conditions for snorkeling and scuba diving. ⁹Indeed, Costa Rica is a wonderful place to go if you love the outdoors.

Questions on the Model

1. What is the title of this paragraph?
2. What is the topic sentence? What information does it give you?
3. How many supporting sentences are there?
4. How many reasons are given? What words introduce these reasons?
5. How many examples are given for each reason? What words tell you that these are examples?
6. What is the concluding sentence?
7. What kind of organizational pattern did the writer use in this paragraph—space order, time order, or listing order?

---

¹**ashore:** on the shore, on the beach

Outlines with Details

In previous chapters, you practiced making simple outlines with main points A, B, C, and so on. In this chapter, you will add details to your main points.

1. Give main points (reasons) capital letters: A, B, C, and so on.
2. Give examples for A, B, and C numbers: 1, 2, 3, and so on.
3. Give examples for 1, 2, and 3 small letters: a, b, c, and so on.
4. Indent each kind of letter or number.

The following model outline has two main points (A, B) and two levels of details: 1, 2 and a, b.

MODEL

Detailed Outline

TOPIC SENTENCE	**Costa Rica**
	Costa Rica is a great place to spend a vacation for two reasons.
1ST REASON	A. Excellent system of national parks—visitors can observe nature
EXAMPLE FOR A	1. Tortuguero National Park
EXAMPLE FOR 1	a. Sea turtle nests
EXAMPLE FOR 1	b. Baby turtles
EXAMPLE FOR A	2. Santa Rosa National Park
EXAMPLE FOR 2	a. Unusual birds—toucans and quetzals
EXAMPLE FOR 2	b. Exotic animals—spider monkeys
2ND REASON	B. Beautiful beaches
EXAMPLE FOR B	1. Beaches at Manuel Antonio National Park
EXAMPLE FOR B	2. Beaches on Cañoa and Cocos Islands
EXAMPLE FOR 2	a. Snorkeling
EXAMPLE FOR 2	b. Scuba diving
CONCLUDING SENTENCE	Costa Rica is a wonderful place to go if you love the outdoors.

Reasons and Examples

When you write a topic sentence such as *Costa Rica is a great place to visit*, or *Women should be jet fighter pilots*, you need to support it with **reasons**. You need to explain *why* Costa Rica is a great place to visit, or *why* women should be jet fighter pilots. The writer of the model paragraph gave two main reasons why tourists enjoy visiting Costa Rica:

1. It has many national parks where tourists can see nature.
2. It has beautiful beaches.

After you state your reasons, you need to support them. A good way to support reasons is to give **specific examples**. In the model paragraph, each of the reasons has two supporting examples. The examples are specific. They are the actual names of places: Tortuguero National Park, Santa Rosa National Park, Manuel Antonio National Park, Cañoa Island, and Cocos Island. Other specific examples in the paragraph are the names of birds (toucans and quetzals) and of an animal (spider monkeys).

PRACTICE 1

Specific Examples

A. Work with a partner. Think of two specific examples for each reason in Outline A.

Outline A

TOPIC SENTENCE   <u>Joe's Diner is the best restaurant in town.</u>

1ST REASON   A. The food is delicious.

EXAMPLE   1. <u>Joe's double cheeseburger is juicy and full of flavor.</u>

EXAMPLE   2. _____

2ND REASON   B. The service is fast and cheerful.

EXAMPLE   1. _____

EXAMPLE   2. _____

3RD REASON   C. The prices are low.

EXAMPLE   1. _____

EXAMPLE   2. _____

CONCLUDING SENTENCE   When you are hungry and in a hurry, try Joe's Diner for a fast, delicious, inexpensive meal served with a smile.

B. For Outline B, think of both reasons and examples.

Outline B

TOPIC SENTENCE   Pete's Pizzeria is the worst fast-food restaurant in town.

1ST REASON   A. _____

EXAMPLE   1. _____

EXAMPLE   2. _____

2ND REASON   B. _____

EXAMPLE   1. _____

EXAMPLE   2. _____

3RD REASON   C. _____

EXAMPLE   1. _____

EXAMPLE   2. _____

CONCLUDING SENTENCE   For slow service and expensive pizza with cardboard crust and rubber cheese, always go to Pete's.

C. Organize the scrambled sentences for each of the following topics into an outline. The sentences are reasons, examples or other specific details, topic sentences, or concluding sentences. Write your outlines on a separate piece of paper.

Topic 1: Reasons *not* to own a Hummer[1]

1. To sum up, for the health of your bank balance as well as for the health of the environment, don't buy a Hummer.
2. Hummers are big gas hogs.[2]
3. The H2 model gets less than 10 miles per gallon of gas.
4. In one year, a Hummer gives off 24,100 pounds of carbon dioxide, which is two to three times more than average cars give off.
5. There are at least two reasons for not buying the huge, military-type vehicle called a Hummer.
6. The U.S. government's Environmental Protection Agency gives it a failing grade.
7. When gas costs $3 per gallon, it costs $100 to fill up a Hummer's big gas tank.
8. Hummers are bad for the environment.

Topic 2: Reasons to own a Smart[3]

1. The Smart is easy on the wallet.[4]
2. The Smart will be the next "cool" car to own for several reasons.
3. The design is eye-catching.
4. It costs between $15,000 and $25,000.
5. It has changeable door panels in stylish colors.
6. It is only 8 feet, 2½ inches (250 cm) long, which is the width of a street parking space.
7. Its body is modern in design.
8. You can park two or three Smarts side-by-side in a single street parking space.

---

[1]Information from "Top Ten Reasons Not to Buy a Hummer," Code Pink: Women for Peace, http://www. codepink4peace.org/article.php?id=86 and "Green Vehicle Guide," U.S. Environmental Protection Agency, http://www.eps.gov/greenvehicles/E-HUMMER-H2-06.htm (accessed October 23, 2006).
[2]**gas hogs:** automobiles that use a lot of gas (A hog is a male pig.)
[3]Information from John Gartner, "Small Car Seeks Small Niche," Wired News, May 3, 2005, http://wired. com/news/autotech/0,2554,67405,00.html (accessed July 8, 2006) and Philip Reed, "The Smart Invasion: A New Smart Line of Cars Is Coming to the U.S.," Edmunds.com, March 9, 2004, http://www.edmunds.com/ advice/specialreports/articles/101361/article.html (accessed October 23, 2006).
[4]**easy on the wallet:** economical (idiom)

9. The European model gets 60 miles per gallon of gas, and the U.S. model 50 miles per gallon.
10. The Smart is easy to park.
11. For style, economy, and easy parking, the Smart is the car to buy.

Transition Signals with Reasons

When you give reasons, you should introduce each one with a transition signal. Use the listing-order transition signals: *first, first of all, second, third, finally,* and so forth.

Pattern 1	**First of all,** _____.
	Second, _____.

First of all, Costa Rica has an excellent system of national parks.

Second, Costa Rica has many beautiful beaches.

You can also put the transition word in the subject (without commas), like this:

Pattern 2	The **first** reason is _____.
	The **second** reason is _____.

There are two ways to complete the Pattern 2 sentences above.

- With a noun phrase:[5]

  The first reason is **the excellent system of national parks.**

  The second reason is **Costa Rica's beautiful beaches.**

- With a sentence connected by *that*:

  The first reason is **that Costa Rica has an excellent system of national parks.**

  The second reason is **that Costa Rica has many beautiful beaches.**

Remember: Don't use a comma when the transition signal is included in the subject.

---

[5]**noun phrase:** a group of words ending with a noun that belong together in meaning: *the old house, a good book, several friends*

Conclusion Signals with Reasons

In addition to the conclusion signals such as *Indeed* and *To sum up* that you have already learned, you can begin a concluding sentence with *For these (two, three, four,* and so on) *reasons*, followed by a sentence.

> **For these** _____ **reasons,** _____ .

> **For these two reasons,** Costa Rica is a wonderful place to go if you love the outdoors.

Another way to write a concluding sentence is to begin it with *Because of*, followed by one or more noun phrases.

> **Because of** _____ , _____
> _____ .

> **Because of its national parks and beautiful beaches,** Costa Rica is a wonderful place to go if you love the outdoors.

PRACTICE 2

Transition Signals with Reasons

Here are three more reasons that Costa Rica is a good place to visit. Rewrite each reason twice to add transition signals.

Step 1 On the first line (a), rewrite the sentence and use a listing-order transition signal as in the **a** example for Reason 3 below. Be sure to use a comma.

Step 2 On the second line (b), rewrite the sentence and include the transition signal in the subject as in the **b** example. Don't use a comma.

Reason 3:

San Jose, the capital, has a pleasant climate.

a. Third, San Jose, the capital, has a pleasant climate.

b. A third reason is that San Jose, the capital, has a pleasant
     climate.

Reason 4:

Hotels and restaurants are inexpensive.

a. _____

b. _____

Reason 5:

The people are friendly to tourists.

a. _____

b. _____

Transition Signals with Examples

There are three transition signals to introduce examples: *for example, for instance*, and *such as*. Notice the two different punctuation patterns used with them.

Use *For example* and *For instance* when your example is a complete sentence. The two transition signals have exactly the same meaning. Put them at the beginning of the sentence and follow them with a comma.[1]

Pattern 1	**For example,** _____ (+ *sentence*)
	For instance, _____ (+ *sentence*)

For example, visitors can watch sea turtles come ashore to lay their eggs in the sand in Tortuguero National Park.

For instance, visitors can watch sea turtles come ashore to lay their eggs in the sand in Tortuguero National Park.

Use *such as, for example*, and *for instance* in the middle of a sentence when your example is a noun or a list of nouns that appear at the end of the sentence.

Pattern 2	_____, **such as** _____ (+ *nouns*)
	_____, **for example,** _____ (+ *nouns*)
	_____, **for instance,** _____ (+ *nouns*)

- Put a comma before *such as*.[2]

  Visitors can see rare birds, **such as** toucans and quetzals.

- Put a comma before and after *for example* and *for instance*.

  Visitors can see rare birds, **for example,** toucans and quetzals.

  Visitors can see rare birds, **for instance,** toucans and quetzals.

---

[1]*For example* and *for instance* can also be inserted into the middle or added to the end of an example that is a complete sentence.

[2]Sometimes *such as* appears without commas. The rule for using commas with *such as* has to do with restrictive and nonrestrictive structures, which will be introduced in Chapter 6.

> ### Writer's Tip
>
> Be careful when you begin a sentence with *For example* or *For instance*. Make sure your sentence follows either Pattern 1 or Pattern 2.
>
> WRONG: The restaurant specializes in shellfish. For example, fresh lobster and crab.
>
> RIGHT: The restaurant specializes in shellfish. For example, it serves fresh lobster and crab. (Pattern 1)
>
> RIGHT: The restaurant specializes in shellfish, such as fresh lobster and crab. (Pattern 2)
>
> RIGHT: The restaurant specializes in shellfish, for example, fresh lobster and crab. (Pattern 2)

PRACTICE 3

Transition Signals with Examples

A. Add commas to the following sentences.

1. Denmark has many attractions for children such as Tivoli Gardens and Legoland.

2. Japan is famous for its beautiful gardens. For example the rock garden of Ryoanji Temple is known all over the world.

3. In São Paulo, there is a mix of architecture. You can see traditional architecture in some buildings for example the Martinelli Building and Banco do Estado de São Paulo.

4. There are also many modern buildings in São Paulo. For instance the Banco Sumitomo and Conjunto Nacional are very modern in design.

5. Bolivia offers tourists many interesting places to visit for instance the capital city of La Paz and the islands in Lake Titicaca.

B. Fill in the blanks with *for example, for instance*, or *such as*. Add commas where necessary. (There may be more than one correct answer.)

1. San Francisco has several ethnic[1] neighborhoods _____ North Beach (Italian), the Mission District (Hispanic), and Chinatown (Chinese).

2. When you visit the ethnic neighborhoods of Miami, you feel that you are in a foreign country. _____ in Little Havana you can easily imagine that you are in Cuba.

---

[1]**ethnic:** of different cultures, races, and nationalities

3. Summers are much cooler in San Francisco than in Los Angeles.

   _____ the average July temperature in San Francisco is about 65°F, but it is 85°F in Los Angeles.

4. Mexico's Yucatan Peninsula has many luxury beach resorts

   _____ Cancún and Cozumel.

5. The Yucatan is full of archaeological treasures _____ the Mayan ruins at Chichen Itza and Tulum.

Try It Out! Write a paragraph recommending your school as a place to study English. Use the reasons and examples that you developed in the Prewriting Activity at the beginning of the chapter. Complete the steps in the writing process.

Step 2 Write the first draft.

- Write ROUGH DRAFT at the top of your paper.
- Use the same topic sentence as in your outline, and add a concluding sentence.
- Use transition signals for your main points and for your examples. Try to use *for example, for instance,* and *such as* at least once.

Step 3 Edit the first draft.

- Edit your paragraph with a partner as you have done in previous chapters. Use the Reader's Response 5A and Writer's Self-Check 5A on pages 206 and 207.

Step 4 Write the final copy.

- Write a neat final copy of your paragraph to hand in to your teacher. Your teacher may also ask you to hand in your prewriting, your outline, and your other drafts.

PART 2 | Sentence Structure

More About Complex Sentences

In Chapter 3, you learned about complex sentences with dependent time clauses. Now let's study other kinds of dependent clauses. First, review these five points:

- An independent clause is a sentence by itself.
- A dependent clause is not a sentence by itself. A dependent clause needs an independent clause to complete its meaning.

> **Independent clause**   The class ended.
>
> **Dependent clause**   . . . when the class ended . . .

- A complex sentence is one independent clause and one or more dependent clauses.
- The clauses can be in any order.
- Put a comma after a dependent clause when the dependent clause comes before an independent clause.

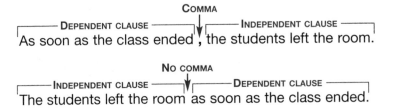

Reason and Condition Subordinators

In Chapter 3, you practiced writing sentences with time subordinators. Here are two other kinds. One kind tells a reason for something to happen, and the other kind states a condition for something to happen.

Reason Subordinators	
because	They canceled the game **because** the field was too wet.
since	**Since** the field was too wet, they canceled the game.

Condition Subordinator	
if	John is unhappy **if** he doesn't get an A in every class.

Here are some things to know about these subordinators.

1. *Because* and *since* have exactly the same meaning, and there is no difference in their use.

   Because Tina is good at math, she decided to become an engineer.

   Since Tina is good at math, she decided to become an engineer.

   Tina decided to become an engineer **because** she is good at math.

   Tina decided to become an engineer **since** she is good at math.

2. The word *since* can be either a reason subordinator or a time subordinator.

> **Since** I don't own a car, I take the bus to school. (*reason*)
>
> **Since** Eddie started lifting weights, he has become much stronger. (*time*)

3. *Because* is a subordinator. *Because of* is a two-word preposition.

> Hawaii is a popular vacation spot **because of** its beautiful beaches. (*preposition*)
>
> Hawaii is a popular vacation spot **because** it has beautiful beaches. (*subordinator*)

4. *If* introduces a condition. (*Note*: Sentences with conditional clauses often require special combinations of verb tenses. Consult a grammar book for information.)

> **If** you don't practice, you won't learn as quickly.
>
> **If** you cook chicken too long, it becomes tough and dry.
>
> Don't open an email **if** you don't know the sender.

PRACTICE 4

Complex Sentences

A. Analyze these complex sentences.

Step 1 Underline the independent clauses with a <u>solid line</u> and the dependent clauses with a <u>broken line</u>.

Step 2 Draw a circle around the subordinator.

Step 3 Add a comma if one is needed.

1. <u>Tourists love to visit Arizona</u> (because) <u>it has many interesting things to do and see</u>.
2. Since summers are hot in Arizona the best time to go there is the spring or fall.
3. If you are interested in Native Americans you should visit the Navajo and Hopi reservations[1] in northern Arizona.
4. You might be able to visit a tribal fair[2] if you are lucky.
5. The Navajo call themselves a "nation" because they govern themselves.
6. Because the Navajo language is so difficult the U.S. military used it for secret messages during World War II.

(continued on next page)

---

[1]**reservations:** areas of land in the U.S. kept separate for Native Americans to live on
[2]**tribal fair:** an outdoor event where Native Americans celebrate their culture

B. Complete the dependent clause to make a complex sentence.

1. I enjoy traveling because _I like to learn about new cultures_ .

2. I take a trip whenever _____.

3. After _____, I plan to work my way around the world.

4. Before _____, I want to see as much of the world as possible.

5. I have to travel now because _____.

6. If _____ I want to spend at least one year on the road.[1]

PRACTICE 5

*Editing
Sentence and
Punctuation
Errors*

Step 1 Look for sentence and punctuation errors in the following paragraph. You should find two comma errors, two fragments, one run-on, and one comma splice.

Step 2 In the lines below, rewrite the incorrect sentences correctly.

Soccer

[1]Soccer is truly the world's most popular sport. [2]Since the game began in England about 150 years ago it has spread to every corner of the globe. [3]Millions of people go to soccer stadiums to watch their favorite team. [4]While millions more watch on television. [5]One reason for soccer's popularity may be its economy and simplicity. [6]Anyone can afford to play soccer, because it doesn't require expensive equipment. [7]Also, has simple rules. [8]Soccer is the number one sport in most of the world, it is not the most popular sport in North America. [9]Ice hockey is the favorite in Canada American football is the favorite in the United States. [10]However, soccer is gaining new players and fans in those countries too.

Corrected Sentences:

_____

_____

_____

_____

_____

_____

_____

_____

_____

---

[1]**on the road:** traveling (idiom)

Try It Out!

Step 1 Combine the sentences in each group to make one sentence. Some of your sentences will be simple, some will be compound, and some will be complex. If there is only one sentence, do not change it but simply copy it. Punctuate each sentence carefully.

Step 2 Write the sentences together as a paragraph. Add an appropriate transition signal where suggested.

My Love-Hate Relationship with Camping

1. a. There are two reasons I love camping.
   b. There are two reasons I hate camping.

2. a. Living outdoors for a few days refreshes my mind.
   b. Living outdoors for a few days renews my spirit.
      (*Add a transition signal to 2a.*)

3. a. I have spent a few days in nature.
   b. I feel free again.
   c. I feel happy again.
      (*Use* after *in front of 3a.*)

4. a. Camping brings my family closer together.
   b. Everyone helps plan the trip.
   c. Everyone helps set up the campsite.
   d. Everyone helps prepare the meals.
      (*Add a transition signal to 4a. Use* because *in front of 4b.*)

5. On the other hand, sometimes I hate camping.

6. I don't sleep well. (*Add a transition signal.*)

7. a. I hate to sleep on the ground.
   b. The ground is hard.
      (*Use* because *in front of 7b.*)

8. a. I get up in the morning.
   b. I can hardly move.
      (*Use* when *in front of 8a.*)

9. a. My back hurts.
   b. My muscles ache.

(continued on next page)

10. a. The second reason I hate camping is this.
    b. We always forget something important.
    (*Replace the word* this *with the subordinating word* that *and combine the sentences.*)

11. a. We forgot to bring our tent.
    b. This happened last year.
    c. We had to sleep in the open.[1]
    (*Use* so *in front of 11c.*)

12. a. I didn't sleep at all.
    b. I am afraid of snakes.
    c. I am afraid of bugs.
    (*Use* because *in front of 12b.*)

13. a. I see a snake.
    b. I see a bug.
    c. I am frozen with fear.
    (*Use* if *in front of 13a.*)

14. a. Why do I continue to go camping?
    b. I have such a love-hate relationship with it.
    (*Use* when *in front of 15b. Your combined sentence will be a question.*)

My Love-Hate Relationship with Camping

There are two reasons I love camping and two reasons I hate camping.

_____

_____

_____

_____

_____

_____

_____

_____

_____

_____

_____

_____

---

[1] **in the open:** outside, without shelter

_____

_____

_____

_____

_____

_____

_____

PART 3 | Capitalization and Punctuation

In this section, you will learn more about capitalization and using commas.

Capitalization:
Two More
Rules

Here are two more capitalization rules.

Rules	Examples
Capitalize:	
11. Some abbreviations.	**IBM** **UN** **UCLA** **VW** **TV** **CBS** **USA** **UAE** **UK**
NOTE 1: USA is an abbreviation for United States of America. Do not capitalize all of the letters in a country's name.	**U**nited **S**tates of **A**merica **S**audi **A**rabia **J**apan
NOTE 2: Capitalize only the first letter of the abbreviation of a person's title.	**D**r. **M**r. and **M**rs. **P**rof.
12. All the words in a greeting and the first word in the closing of a letter.	**D**ear **S**ir: **T**o **W**hom **I**t **M**ay **C**oncern: **L**ove, **V**ery truly yours,

PRACTICE 6

Capitalization Review

Change the small letters to capital letters wherever necessary in the letter from Nicole to her sister Miki. To review the rules you learned earlier, turn back to pages 17 and 89.

---

september 3, 20__

dear miki,

well, here i am in new york city. i still can't believe that i'm actually here! i arrived on saturday after a long flight from paris on air france. the food was excellent, and so was the movie. we saw <u>gone with the wind</u>. i stayed saturday and sunday nights at the fairmount hotel near rockefeller center. then on monday i moved into my dormitory at nyu.[1]

i spent my entire first weekend here sightseeing. i saw many famous places: rockefeller center, the united nations, the guggenheim museum, the ny stock exchange, and the statue of liberty. i window-shopped at gucci and saks fifth avenue. i also visited another famous art museum and the nbc television studios.

today is a holiday in the united states. it is labor day, so all government offices, schools, and banks are closed. people in the united states celebrate the end of summer by having a three-day weekend. many new yorkers spend the day in central park or go to the beach on long island.

i learned some interesting things about new york. its nickname is "the big apple," but no one knows why it's called an apple and not a banana or an orange. another interesting fact is that the first europeans who came here bought manhattan island[2] from the natives for only $24. of course, it's now worth trillions of dollars.

well, that's all for now. classes begin next week. i'm having a good time, but i miss you all, and i really miss french food. write soon.

with love,

nicole

---

[1]**NYU:** New York University
[2]**Manhattan Island:** the island on which part of New York City is located

Commas: Four More Rules So far, you have learned these four comma rules:

Rules	Examples
Use a comma:	
1. After transition signals and prepositional phrases at the beginning of a sentence (except *then*).	First, carry out the empty bottles and cans. From my window, I have a beautiful view. After lunch, my grandfather takes a nap. For example, some teachers give pop quizzes.
2. Before coordinating conjunctions in a compound sentence.	Cook the rice over low heat for twenty minutes, but don't let it burn. Many students work, so they don't have time to do homework.
3. In a complex sentence when a dependent adverb clause comes before an independent clause.	Because Mexico City is surrounded by mountains, it has a lot of smog.
4. To separate items in a series.	In our class there are students from Mexico, Japan, Vietnam, Iran, China, and Guatemala.

Here are four more comma rules:

Rules	Examples
Use a comma:	
5. To separate thousands, millions, billions, etc. BUT NOT in a number that expresses a year or an address, and NOT to separate dollars from cents or whole numbers from decimals. (Use a period, not a comma.)	The college has 23,250 students. in the year 2010 2935 Main Street $59.95 $6\frac{7}{8} = 6.875$
6. To separate the parts of dates and after years in the middle of a sentence.	The third millennium started on January 1, 2001, not on January 1, 2000.
7. To separate the parts of a U.S. address EXCEPT between the state and the zip code when the address is in a sentence. In the address of letters and on envelopes, do not use commas.	The address of the White House is 1600 Pennsylvania Avenue, Washington, DC 20500.
8. After the greeting and closing in a personal letter, and after the closing in a business letter.	Dear Michiko, Love, Dear Mom, Very truly yours,

PRACTICE 7

Commas

A. Add commas to the sentences. (Not all sentences need them.)

Rules 1–4

1. Some students work full time and go to school part time.

2. For example one of my classmates takes six units and works forty hours a week.

3. Since he is also married and has two children he is a very busy person.

4. He works at night attends class in the morning and sleeps when he can.

5. When he fell asleep in class yesterday we decided not to wake him up.

6. Scientists believe that animals can think feel and communicate just as humans can.

7. My dog certainly acts like a human at times.

8. For instance when he does something bad he looks guilty.

9. He hangs his head drops his tail and looks up at me with sad eyes.

10. Later we usually discover the reason for his guilty looks but it's hard to punish him.

Rules 1–7

11. China is the country with the largest population, but with a land area of 17075400 square kilometers, Russia is the largest country in size.

12. My mother lives in Miami Florida in the winter and in Denver Colorado in the summer.

13. When it becomes too hot in Florida she moves to Colorado.

14. She moves back to Florida when it gets too cold in Colorado.

15. Her address in Florida is P.O. Box 695 Miami Florida 33167 and her address in Colorado is 3562 State Street Apt. 3-C Denver Colorado 80210.

16. On Sunday June 10 2007 I graduated from college.

17. Then on Monday June 11 2007 I started looking for a job.

B. Work by yourself and then with a partner. Write one sentence of your own for Rules 1–7, but leave out the commas. Then give your seven sentences to your partner and ask him or her to put in the commas.

1. _____

    _____

2. _____

    _____

3. _____

    _____

4. _____

    _____

5. _____

    _____

6. _____

    _____

7. _____

    _____

PART 4 | Writing

**Review
Questions**

Review the important points in this chapter by answering the following questions.

Organization

1. Which pattern of organization is best to use in a paragraph that gives reasons: time order or listing order?
2. What three transition signals introduce examples?
3. Which two examples signals can you use at the beginning of a sentence?
4. Which ones can you use in the middle of a sentence to introduce a series of nouns?

Sentence Structure

5. What two subordinators can you use to introduce a reason?
6. What subordinator can you use to introduce a condition?
7. How do you punctuate a complex sentence?

Capitalization and Punctuation

8. What two new capitalization rules did you learn in this chapter?
9. What four new comma rules did you learn in this chapter?

Writing Assignment

Imagine that you work for a travel agency. Write a paragraph recommending your hometown, the place where you live now, or any place that you know well as a place to go on vacation. Give at least three reasons why a visitor would enjoy vacationing there. Give specific examples for your reasons. Use the paragraph about Costa Rica on page 124 as a model.

Step 1 Prewrite to get ideas.

- Get ideas by using the freewriting, listing, or clustering technique.
- Find two to four reasons and at least one specific example for each reason. The more examples you give, the better your paragraph will be.
- Organize your reasons and examples by making an outline. Make your outline as detailed as possible. It should be similar to the outline on page 125.

Step 2 Write the first draft.

- Write ROUGH DRAFT at the top of your paper.
- Be sure to use transition signals.
- Pay attention to sentence structure. Try to write a variety of sentence types: simple, compound, and complex.

Step 3 Edit the first draft.

- Edit your paragraph with a partner as you have done in previous chapters. Use the Reader's Response 5B and Writer's Self-Check 5B on pages 208 and 209.

Step 4 Write the final draft.

- Write a neat final draft to hand in to your teacher. Your teacher may also ask you to hand in your prewriting, your outline, and your other drafts.

Expressing Your Opinion

Chapter Preview

Prewriting Activity: Getting Ideas from Reading

Part 1: Organization

Opinion Paragraphs

Part 2: Sentence Structure

Adjective Clauses with *who, which,* and *that*

More About Fragments

Part 3: Punctuation

Quotation Marks

Part 4: Writing

Chapter Preview

In this chapter, you will write a paragraph in which you express an **opinion** and support it. You will also study and practice:

- distinguishing between opinions and facts
- adjective clauses with *who, which,* and *that*
- a different kind of fragment
- quotation marks

Prewriting Activity: Getting Ideas from Reading

Work with a partner or small group.

1. Read the newspaper story on page 147 several times. Make sure you understand all the words and sentences.

2. Then look at the chart on page 148 and discuss this question with your partner or group: Should the judge allow Gregory to divorce his parents?

   - Make a list of *yes* reasons if you agree.
   - Make a list of *no* reasons if you don't agree.
   - Support each reason. As support, use information from the newspaper story and/or use information from your own knowledge and experience.

Here are some points to discuss:

- What kind of parent is Rachel Kingsley?
- Does a biological parent have more rights to his or her child than an adoptive parent?

BOY DIVORCES PARENTS

Twelve-year-old Gregory Kingsley is in court asking a judge to give him a divorce from his natural mother and father. He wants his foster parents,[1] George and Lizabeth Russ, to adopt[2] him.

Gregory's lawyers say that Gregory's natural mother, Rachel Kingsley, has not taken good care of him. They say that she abandoned[3] him because she sent him to live with relatives and foster parents.

Gregory has lived for many years as a foster child. Gregory tells the judge that his mother is cold and doesn't seem to care about him. He says that for many years, his mother sent him no cards, no letters, no Christmas gifts, and no birthday presents.

"I thought she forgot about me," he says.

Other people describe Rachel Kingsley as a person who abuses[4] drugs and alcohol. They say that she spent more time partying with male

Gregory Kingsley

visitors than she spent with Gregory and his two younger brothers. They also say that she sometimes hit the children.

Gregory says that she kept marijuana in a brown box in the living room. He also says, "She stayed out all night and brought her friends home and drank. We never had enough money, and sometimes we didn't have food."

Mrs. Kingsley says she tries to be a good mother. She says she had to send Gregory away for a while because she

didn't have enough money to take care of him. At the time, she didn't have a job. Now she has two jobs, and she is living near her parents, who can help her take care of the children.

She thought it would be better for Gregory to live with a foster family while she was having financial problems, but she never wanted him to be away from her and his brothers permanently. She says, "I thought that if I worked hard, he would be returned to me."

Her lawyer says that Rachel Kingsley's problems were temporary and that she is trying to become a responsible parent. He also says that the rights of a natural family to remain together are stronger than the rights of a foster family.

Her father believes that she has learned from her mistakes and should be given a second chance.

---

[1]**foster parents:** parents who are paid by the government to take care of children when the children's own parents cannot do so
[2]**adopt:** become the legal parents of someone
[3]**abandoned:** left behind
[4]**abuses:** uses in a bad or wrong way

Should the judge allow Gregory to divorce his parents?

YES, the judge should allow Gregory to divorce his mother.	NO, the judge should not allow Gregory to divorce his mother.
A. Reason: _____ _____	A. Reason: _____ _____
Support: _____ _____ _____ _____	Support: _____ _____ _____ _____
B. Reason: _____ _____	B. Reason: _____ _____
Support: _____ _____ _____ _____	Support: _____ _____ _____ _____
C. Reason: _____ _____	C. Reason: _____ _____
Support: _____ _____ _____ _____	Support: _____ _____ _____ _____

PART 1 | Organization

Opinion Paragraphs

In everyday life, people have opinions about issues and talk about them. Should smoking be allowed everywhere? Do you agree with restrictions on teenagers during their first year of driving? Should the government ban the sale of handguns?

People also write their opinions. If you look at the "Letters to the Editor" section of any newspaper, you will find letters from people discussing their points of view. In college classes, you often have to express and support your opinions.

There are four keys to writing a successful opinion paragraph.

1. State your opinion clearly in the topic sentence.
2. Explain each reason in logical order.
3. Use facts to support each reason.
4. End with a powerful concluding sentence that your reader will remember.

Facts and Opinions

Opinions are statements of someone's belief. When you say, "I believe . . ." or "I think that . . .," you are expressing your opinion. Opinions are different from facts. People can disagree with opinions. **Facts** are true statements that no one can disagree with.

Read these sentences. Which ones are facts, and which ones are opinions?

The sun rises in the east.	The sunrise was beautiful this morning.
The temperature of the lake is 55°F.	The lake is too cold for swimming.
According to highway accident reports, using a cell phone while driving is dangerous.	Using a cell phone while driving is dangerous.
Women could not vote in the United States until 1920.	Everyone should vote.
Mrs. Kingsley said, "I am a good mother."	Mrs. Kingsley is a good mother.

The sentences on the left side are facts. They are true. Even the last sentence, "Mrs. Kingsley said, 'I am a good mother,' " is a fact. It is a fact that she said this. What she said—"I am a good mother"—is an opinion, but the fact is that Mrs. Kingsley said something. No one can disagree with the fact that she said something.

The sentences in the right column are opinions. People can disagree with them. They may or may not be true.

Of course, you can use opinions as reasons, but your paragraph will be stronger if you support your opinion with facts.

Read the model paragraph that follows and study its organization.

MODEL

Opinion Paragraph

Video Games and Violence

[1]In my opinion, violent video games are harmful to young people. [2]First of all, playing these games can cause changes in the behavior of young people. [3]According to studies by psychologists, frequent players have poorer grades in school. [4]They are also more hostile and act more aggressively toward their teachers and classmates.[1] [5]A second reason that violent video games are harmful to young people is that they make young people less sensitive to violence in the real world. [6]The games make it fun to shoot and kill, and the line between play violence and real violence becomes very thin or disappears entirely. [7]Thirteen-year-old Noah Wilson was stabbed to death by a friend who often played the violent game "Mortal Kombat™." [8]Noah's mother said, "The boy who stabbed him was acting out the part of Cyrex," who is a character in the game.[2] [9]A third reason that violent video games are harmful to young people is that they teach players to use violence to solve problems. [10]If classmates tease you, don't try to work it out—bring a gun to school and shoot them. [11]An extreme example of this kind of thinking resulted in the Columbine High School massacre.[3] [12]Two students shot and killed twelve classmates, a teacher, and themselves at Columbine High School in Colorado. [13]The two young killers were fans of the games "Doom™" and "Wolfenstein 3D™." [14]For these three reasons, I feel that violent video games are harmful to young people and should be controlled—or, even better, banned.[4]

Questions on the Model

1. What is the writer's opinion about violent video games? What phrase does she use to introduce her opinion?
2. How many reasons does she give for her opinion?
3. What order does she use to discuss her reasons?
4. In your opinion, which reason is stronger—the first one or the last one? Why?

---

[1]Craig Anderson and Karen Dill, "Video Games and Aggressive Thoughts, Feelings, and Behavior in the Laboratory and in Life," *Journal of Personality and Social Psychology* 78, no. 4 (2000): 772–790, http://www.apa.org/journals/features/psp784772.pdf (accessed November 3, 2006).
[2]Quotation from a transcript of the television program *Donahue*, July 22, 2002, http://www.lionlamb.org/news_articles/donahue_july_22.htm (accessed November 3, 2006).
[3]**massacre:** murder of many people
[4]**banned:** prohibited, not allowed

PRACTICE 1

Analyzing an Opinion Paragraph

Analyze the model paragraph and determine which supporting details are facts and which are opinions.

Step 1 First, complete the outline for the model paragraph on page 150.

Step 2 Then analyze each supporting sentence or detail and decide if it is a fact or an opinion. Write *fact* or *opinion* in the parentheses at the right of each entry in the outline. Remember that people can disagree with opinions but not with facts.

Video Games and Violence

TOPIC SENTENCE   In my opinion, violent video games are harmful to young people.   (Opinion)

FIRST REASON   A. Playing these games can cause changes in the behavior of   (Opinion) young people.

DETAIL   1. According to psychologists, frequent players have poorer (Fact) grades in school.

DETAIL   2. They are also more hostile and act more aggressively (Fact) toward their teachers and classmates.

SECOND REASON   B. _____ ( )

_____

DETAIL   1. _____ ( )

_____

DETAIL   2. Noah Wilson was stabbed to death by a friend who often (Fact) played the violent game "Mortal Kombat."

DETAIL   3. Noah's mother said, "The boy who stabbed him was acting ( ) out the part of Cyrex."

THIRD REASON   C. _____ ( )

_____

DETAIL   1. _____ ( )

_____

DETAIL   2. Story of the Columbine High School massacre. ( )

DETAIL   3. The two killers were fans of "Doom" and "Wolfenstein 3D." ( )

CONCLUDING SENTENCE   _____

_____

Transition Signals for Opinion Paragraphs

1. When you state an opinion, you should indicate that it is an opinion by using an opinion signal, such as one of these.

In my opinion, . . . (with a comma)	**In my opinion,** everyone should be allowed to own a gun.
In my view, . . . (with a comma)	**In my view,** no one should be allowed to own a gun.
I believe (that) . . . (without a comma)	**I believe that** smoking should not be allowed in public places.
I think (that) . . . (without a comma)	**I think** smokers have rights too.

Notice that the first two opinion signals are followed by commas. The second two do not have commas, and you may omit the connecting word *that*.

2. To give information from an outside source (a book, a newspaper, another person), use *according to* with a comma.

According to X, . . . (with a comma)	**According to Gregory,** his mother never wrote to him or sent him birthday cards.
	According to a story in *Science Today* magazine, the Earth is becoming warmer.
	According to a government report, few Russians have more than one child.

3. In your concluding sentence, you can remind your reader of the number of reasons.

For these (two, three, four, and so on) reasons, . . . (with a comma)	**For these two reasons,** I believe that pesticides are harmful.

If you wish, make a recommendation for action.

For these three reasons, the government should ban the use of all pesticides.

PRACTICE 2

Outlining an Opinion Paragraph

Work by yourself or with a partner. Choose two topics (topics 2, 3, or 4) and complete the outline for each. Use the outline for topic 1 as an example.

Step 1 On the first line, write an opinion topic sentence.

Step 2 Think of two or three reasons for your opinion and write them on the appropriate lines.

Step 3 Think of possible supporting details for each reason, and write them on the appropriate lines.

- Could you take a class survey to get some statistics?
- Could you get a quotation from a classmate or a neighbor?
- Could you use an example from your own personal experience?

Step 4 Write a concluding sentence on the appropriate line.

Example:

1. Topic: Gun control laws

Gun Control Laws

TOPIC SENTENCE — In my opinion, responsible people should be allowed to own a gun.

FIRST REASON — A. Most people need to be able to defend themselves in today's violent society.

POSSIBLE DETAILS — Personal story? News story? Interview classmates/neighbors to get quotations?

SECOND REASON — B. Criminals will always find ways to get guns.

POSSIBLE DETAILS — Bumper sticker: "If guns are outlawed, only outlaws will have guns."

THIRD REASON — C. The U.S. Bill of Rights gives citizens the right to own guns.

POSSIBLE DETAILS — Quotation from the Bill of Rights (Internet or library)

CONCLUDING SENTENCE — For these three reasons, I believe that laws prohibiting gun ownership are wrong.

(continued on next page)

2. Topic: Capital punishment[1]

Capital Punishment

TOPIC SENTENCE _____

_____

FIRST REASON A. _____

_____

POSSIBLE DETAILS _____

_____

SECOND REASON B. _____

_____

POSSIBLE DETAILS _____

_____

THIRD REASON C. _____

_____

POSSIBLE DETAILS _____

_____

CONCLUDING SENTENCE _____

_____

3. Topic: Using cell phones in public places

Using Cell Phones in Public Places

TOPIC SENTENCE _____

_____

FIRST REASON A. _____

_____

POSSIBLE DETAILS _____

_____

---

[1]**capital punishment:** the death penalty

SECOND REASON   B. _____

POSSIBLE DETAILS   _____

THIRD REASON   C. _____

POSSIBLE DETAILS   _____

CONCLUDING SENTENCE   _____

4. Topic: (Your choice)

           (Title) _____

TOPIC SENTENCE   _____

FIRST REASON   A. _____

POSSIBLE DETAILS   _____

SECOND REASON   B. _____

POSSIBLE DETAILS   _____

THIRD REASON   C. _____

POSSIBLE DETAILS   _____

CONCLUDING SENTENCE   _____

Try It Out!   Write a paragraph in which you express and support an opinion about the issue you read about on page 147: Should the judge allow Gregory Kingsley to divorce his mother? Use the reasons and support that you wrote in the chart in the Prewriting Activity at the beginning of the chapter. (Use information from only one side of the chart.) Complete the steps in the writing process.

Step 2 Write the first draft.

- Write ROUGH DRAFT at the top of your paper.
- Begin your paragraph with a topic sentence that expresses your opinion.
- Add transition signals where they are appropriate.
- End your paragraph with a concluding sentence that summarizes your reasons.

Step 3 Edit the first draft.

- Edit your paragraph with a partner as you have done in previous chapters. Use the Reader's Response 6A and Writer's Self-Check 6A on pages 210 and 211.

Step 4 Write the final copy.

- Write a neat final copy to hand in to your teacher. Your teacher may also ask you to hand in your prewriting, your outline, and your other drafts.

PART 2 | Sentence Structure

In this section, you will learn about another kind of dependent clause called an **adjective clause.**[1] As you read the following model, find three sentences containing the word *who* and one sentence containing the word *which*. Underline the sentences.

MODEL

Adjective Clauses

School Uniforms[2]

[1]In my opinion, public school students should wear uniforms. [2]First of all, students who wear uniforms behave better. [3]Long Beach, California, which was one of the first cities in the United States to require uniforms in elementary and middle school, reported increased attendance and decreased bad behavior. [4]In the first year, school crime decreased by 36 percent,

---

[1]Adjective clauses are also called relative clauses.
[2]Supporting details in this paragraph are from Lynne A. Isaacson, "Student Dress Codes," *ERIC Digest* no. 117 (January 1998), http://eric.uoregon.edu/publications/digests/digest117.html (accessed November 8, 2006).

fighting by 51 percent, and vandalism[3] by 18 percent. [5]A second reason for requiring school uniforms is that uniforms increase school spirit. [6]According to a survey taken in South Carolina, middle school students who wear school uniforms have more positive feelings about their schools than students in schools with no uniforms. [7]Third, schools that require uniforms erase economic and social differences. [8]Students from wealthy, middle class, and poor families all wear the same clothes to school, so parents don't feel pressure to spend a lot of money for the latest fashions. [9]Also, students who cannot afford the latest fashions do not feel self-conscious. [10]For these three reasons, I feel that public schools in the United States should require students to wear uniforms, at least in grades K–8.

Questions on the Model

1. How many reasons does the writer give for requiring school uniforms in elementary and middle school?
2. Are all of the reasons supported with facts? Which one(s) are? Which one(s) are not?

Adjective Clauses with *who, which,* and *that*

In earlier chapters, you studied dependent clauses beginning with words such as *because, since, when, after, before,* and *if.* These clauses are called adverb clauses because they act like adverbs. That is, they give more information about a verb.

There is another kind of dependent clause that begins with words such as *who, which,* and *that.* These clauses are called **adjective clauses** because they act like adjectives. That is, they give more information about nouns.

In the following sentences, the adjective clause is underlined with a broken line. There is a circle around *who, which,* or *that* and an arrow points to the noun that the adjective clause gives more information about. Notice that the adjective clause comes directly after that noun.

Students (who) wear uniforms behave better.

Long Beach, California, (which) was one of the first cities in the United States to require uniforms in elementary and middle school, reported increased attendance and decreased bad behavior.

Schools (that) require uniforms erase economic and social differences.

---

[3]**vandalism:** damage such as broken windows and graffiti

Here are some things to know about adjective clauses:

> 1. Adjective clauses begin with the words *who, which,* and *that* (and others).
>   **who** is used for people
>   **which** is used for things
>   **that** is used for things (and for people in informal English)
>
> 2. An adjective clause always follows the noun it gives more information about.
>
> 3. Commas are sometimes used with adjective clauses, and sometimes not. (You will learn about this rule later.)

PRACTICE 3

Adjective Clauses with who, which, *and* that

A. Identify adjective clauses.

Step 1 Underline the adjective clause with a broken line.

Step 2 Circle *who, which,* or *that.*

Step 3 Draw an arrow from *who, which,* or *that* to the noun that the adjective clause gives more information about.

1. Gregory Kingsley, who is twelve years old, wants to divorce his mother.

2. His mother, who neglected him and his brothers, wants to keep him.

3. He wants to be adopted by the Russes, who are his foster parents.

4. Foster parents are people who take care of abused or neglected children.

5. A box that contained marijuana was in the living room.

6. Mrs. Kingsley smoked marijuana, which is an illegal drug.

7. The boys' father, who did not live with their mother, did not want the children to live with him.

8. This case, which was the first child-parent divorce in the United States, received a lot of attention.

9. The lawyer who represented Mrs. Kingsley was a woman.

10. The judge made a decision that most people agree with.[1]

---

[1]The judge allowed Gregory to divorce his parents. The Russes adopted him, and his name is now Shawn Russ.

B. Complete the adjective clause in each sentence.

Step 1 Write *who* or *which* in the space in each sentence. (Do not use *that* in this exercise.)

Step 2 Draw an arrow from *who* or *which* to the noun that the adjective clause gives more information about.

Step 3 Circle the verb in the adjective clause. Is it singular or plural? Is the noun that your arrow points to singular or plural?

Arranged Marriages

1. In arranged marriages, _____which_____ (are) common in many countries, someone else chooses your marriage partner.

2. Sometimes the parents, _____ know their child better than anyone, choose.

3. Sometimes the parents hire a matchmaker, _____ charges a fee to find a suitable² person.

4. The two young people are probably very nervous at their first meeting, _____ usually takes place in the bride's home.

5. In some cultures, a young man or woman _____ doesn't like the parents' or matchmaker's choice may say "no."

6. Marrying for love, _____ is the custom in most Western cultures, does not guarantee happiness.

7. The divorce rate among couples _____ marry for love is very high.

8. People _____ listened only to their hearts sometimes wish they had listened to their heads.

Punctuating Adjective Clauses

In some situations, you use commas with adjective clauses and in some situations, you don't. Using commas depends on whether the information in an adjective clause is necessary to identify the noun or just gives extra information about it.

---

²**suitable:** right or acceptable for a particular situation

Compare the sentences in the following chart:

Extra information	Necessary information
(Use commas)	(Don't use commas)
Rachel Kingsley, <u>who uses drugs</u>, is not a good parent.	A person <u>who uses drugs</u> is not a good parent.

- In the sentence on the left, the adjective clause *who uses drugs* is extra information about Rachel Kingsley. We don't need this information to identify her because her name tells us who she is. If an adjective clause gives extra information, separate it from the rest of the sentence with commas.
- In the sentence on the right, the adjective clause *who uses drugs* is necessary information to identify *person*. Which person is not a good parent?—a person who uses drugs. If the information in an adjective clause is necessary, do not use commas.

Here are more examples:

Extra information	Necessary information
(Use commas)	(Don't use commas)
Children shouldn't play the video game *Grand Theft Auto*, <u>which teaches criminal behavior</u>.	Children shouldn't play video games <u>which/that teach criminal behavior</u>.
Sergio, <u>who is sitting next to the window</u>, isn't paying attention.	The student <u>who is sitting next to the window</u> isn't paying attention.
Let's study at my apartment, <u>which is just a few minutes from campus</u>.	They rented an apartment <u>that/which was close to their child's school</u>.

Writer's Tips

1. Use *that* with necessary clauses only.
2. Never use commas when a clause begins with *that*.

A college major✗that is very popular these days✗is psychology.

A book✗that gives synonyms for words✗is called a thesaurus.

PRACTICE 4

Punctuating Adjective Clauses

A. Punctuate adjective clauses.

Step 1 Underline the adjective clause in each sentence with a broken line.

Step 2 Draw an arrow to the noun that the adjective clause gives more information about.

Step 3 Add commas if necessary.

1. A country that has a king or queen is called a monarchy.

2. England, which has a queen, is a monarchy.

3. A pediatrician is a doctor who takes care of children.

4. Dr. Jones who is our neighbor is a pediatrician.

5. Students who studied got As on the final exam.

6. Gabriela and Trinh who studied got As on the final exam.

7. My birthday is next Monday which is a holiday.

8. A holiday that is especially fun for children is Halloween.

B. Add commas where they are necessary in the following paragraph.

The Story of Coca-Cola

[1]A popular beverage that is sold all over the world is Coca-Cola. [2]A doctor who lived in Atlanta, Georgia, invented it in 1886. [3]Dr. John Pemberton who was also a pharmacist first sold Coca-Cola as a nerve tonic,[1] stimulant[2], and headache medicine. [4]The name of the dark brown syrup that made people feel better was "Pemberton's French Wine Coca." [5]Later someone added soda water to the syrup and it became the beverage that is our modern Coca-Cola. [6]The first part of the name (*coca*) comes from *cocaine* which was one of the original ingredients. [7]The second part of the name (*cola*) comes from *kola nut* which is still an ingredient. [8]The original formula has changed over the years. [9]Of course Coca-Cola no longer contains cocaine which is an illegal drug but it still tastes delicious. [10]The formula for Coca-Cola is a secret that is carefully guarded.

Complex Sentences with Adjective Clauses

In the next practices, you will write sentences with adjective clauses. Remember that an adjective clause is a dependent clause. Therefore, you must combine it with an independent clause to make a complex sentence.

---

[1]**tonic:** something that gives you energy
[2]**stimulant:** something that stimulates, gives you energy (similar to *tonic*)

PRACTICE 5

Sentences with Adjective Clauses

A. Choose an adjective clause from the list on the right and combine it with an independent clause from the left. Several different combinations are possible. Be sure to put the adjective clause directly after the noun it gives more information about, and add commas if necessary. Write your new sentences on the lines below.

Independent Clauses

1. They gave their boss a Rolex watch.

2. The purse is hers.

3. Alice moved to New York last month.

4. She is living in an apartment.

5. On our honeymoon, we stayed at the Bellagio.

6. Uncle John has everything.

7. A person has everything.

Adjective Clauses

a. who owns a house on every continent, his own private jet, and two yachts

b. which has a view of Central Park

c. who was celebrating his fiftieth birthday

d. who has love

e. who is my best friend

f. that is lying under the chair

g. which is our favorite hotel in Las Vegas

1. _They gave their boss, who was celebrating his fiftieth birthday, a Rolex watch._

2. _____

3. _____

4. _____

5. _____

6. _____

7. _____

B. Combine two simple sentences to make a complex sentence containing an adjective clause.

Step 1 Read the two sentences in each pair. Which noun in the first sentence is the second sentence talking about? Find it and underline it. Notice whether it is a person or a thing.

Step 2 Change the second sentence into an adjective clause by crossing out the subject and substituting *who, which,* or *that*.

Step 3 Write a combined sentence. Move the new adjective clause to its correct position (right after the underlined noun) in the first sentence.

Step 4 Add commas if necessary.

Cultures in Conflict

1. <u>Jamila Haddad</u> ran away from home last week. ~~Jamila~~ *who (person)* is a high school student in Chicago.

     Jamila Haddad, who is a high school student in Chicago, ran away from home last week.

2. She ran away to avoid <u>a marriage</u>. ~~The marriage~~ *which OR that (thing)* was arranged by her parents.

     She ran away to avoid a marriage which (or that) was arranged by her parents.

3. Mr. and Mrs. Haddad are very traditional. Mr. and Mrs. Haddad are from Lebanon.

     _____

     _____

4. Jamila is the oldest daughter in the Haddad family. The Haddad family immigrated to this country seven years ago.

     _____

     _____

5. Her parents want her to marry a man. The man is thirty-two years old.

     _____

     _____

6. The husband-to-be lives in Lebanon. Lebanon is a country in the Middle East.

     _____

     _____

(continued on next page)

7. He owns a business. The business is very successful.

_____

_____

8. People say that he is very nice. People know him.

_____

_____

9. Jamila ran away from home rather than marry the man. She wants to go to college in her new country.

_____

_____

10. Mr. and Mrs. Haddad don't understand why she ran away. Mr. and Mrs. Haddad thought they had arranged a good future for their daughter.

_____

_____

C. Unscramble the following definitions. Each unscrambled sentence will contain an adjective clause. Do not add commas. Look up unfamiliar words in a dictionary.

1. A hermit/who/a/person/alone/lives/is

    _A hermit is a person who lives alone._____

2. Carrots/vegetables/are/which/in color/orange/are

    _____

3. A vegetarian/person/doesn't eat/meat/is/a/who

    _____

4. A hybrid/automobile/gasoline/and/which/an/is/runs/on/electricity

    _____

5. Orphans/have/who/parents/no/children/are

    _____

6. A giant panda/animal/lives/that/in/China/an/is

    _____

7. An ichthyologist/scientist/fish/studies/who/is/a/

    _____

For items 8–12, write your own definitions. Use the given words in your definition.

8. chicken/eggs

   A chicken is an animal that lays eggs.

9. cow/milk

   _____

10. jockey/horses

    _____

11. dental hygienist/teeth

    _____

12. eel/fish

    _____

D. Work with a partner or with a group on this exercise.

Step 1 Read the story on page 166. Make sure that you understand all the words. Discuss it with your partner or group.

Step 2 Take information from the story and complete each sentence by finishing the adjective clause. Remember to make the verb in the adjective clause agree (singular or plural) with the noun it gives more information about.

1. Nathan Warmack, who _is a high school student in Jackson, Missouri,_ wanted to wear a kilt to a school dance.

2. A kilt, which _____, is traditional men's clothing from Scotland.

3. Warmack became interested in his Scottish heritage after seeing the movie *Braveheart*, which _____ _____.

4. The vice-principal, who _____, _____ didn't tell him not to wear it.

5. Rick McClard, who _____, _____ told him to change into a pair of pants.

6. Scottish heritage organizations, which _____ _____, are collecting items of clothing to complete his outfit.

(continued on next page)

TEEN VERSUS SCHOOL DRESS CODE[1]

Student Can't Wear Scottish Kilt to School Dance

In 2005, high school senior Nathan Warmack wanted to honor his Scottish heritage[2] by wearing a kilt[3] to a high school dance in Jackson, Missouri. A kilt is the traditional clothing of Scottish men. It looks like a skirt. At the dance, the principal[4] told him to change into a pair of pants. Warmack refused. He said that the kilt was recognizing his heritage.

The issue started a national debate about freedom, symbols, and cultural dress.[5] More than 1,600 people have signed a petition[6] seeking an apology for the student. Scottish organizations support him also. They are gathering articles of clothing—boots, socks, and so on—to complete his outfit.

The issue is not new. In 1992, a high school principal in Texas ordered two boys to put on "more appropriate" clothing when they wore kilts to school. In 1993, a student in the state of Georgia was not allowed into a school dance because he wore a kilt.

Warmack became interested in his family's Scottish origins after seeing the Hollywood movie *Braveheart*. The movie is about a Scottish hero who fought to free Scotland from English rule in the thirteenth century. Young Warmack began reading about Scottish history and researching his family's genealogy. He also bought a kilt and showed it to a vice-principal at his school before the dance. The vice-principal joked about it with him but did not say he couldn't wear it. Warmack and his date arrived at the dance, and Principal Rick McClard told him to go home and change clothes. When Warmack refused, McClard allegedly[7] said, "This is my dance, and I'm not going to have students coming into it looking like clowns."

Several Scottish heritage organizations are angry. They say that the kilt is a symbol of Scottish pride and is considered to be formal dress. "To say the traditional Scottish dress makes you look like a clown is a direct insult to people of Scottish heritage and those who live in Scotland," said Tom Wilson. Wilson is a member of one of the organizations.

---

[1] Associated Press, "Teen Seeks Dress Code Change: Principal Sparks Debate After Telling Student to Wear Pants at School Dance," MSNBC.com, December 22, 2005, http://www.msnbc.msn.com/id/10570399 (accessed November 25, 2006).
[2] **heritage:** ethnic or national origin
[3] **kilt:** traditional clothing of Scottish men; it looks like a skirt
[4] **principal:** the head of a school
[5] **dress:** In this story, the meaning of *dress* is *clothes* or *clothing* in general. It does not mean the particular item of clothing worn by women.
[6] **petition:** written request asking for something
[7] **allegedly:** adverb used when reporting something that other people say is true but that has not been proved

More About Fragments

In Chapter 3, you learned about the sentence error called a fragment. Sometimes this error happens when you write a dependent clause and forget to add an independent clause.

FRAGMENT: If you want to transfer to a four-year college.

FRAGMENT: Because it was raining when we left.

Here is another kind of sentence fragment.

FRAGMENT: Ron, who also takes night classes.

FRAGMENT: The book that was on the table.

In these fragments also, there is no independent clause. There is only a noun and an adjective clause. There are two ways to correct this kind of fragment.

1. Finish the independent clause.

CORRECTED: Ron, who also takes night classes, is very busy.

CORRECTED: The book that was on the table belongs to the teacher.

2. Delete *who, which,* or *that* to make a simple sentence.

CORRECTED: Ron takes night classes.

CORRECTED: The book was on the table.

Writer's Tip

When you fix this kind of fragment by deleting *who, which,* or *that*, be sure the remaining words make a meaningful sentence. For example, this is a fragment:

Pedestrians who cross the street.

If you delete *who*, you get "Pedestrians cross the street." This is not a very interesting or meaningful sentence. It is better to correct this fragment by finishing the independent clause:

Pedestrians who cross the street should look in both directions before stepping off the curb.

PRACTICE 6

Fragments

Step 1 Read each sentence. Decide if it is a fragment or a sentence. Write *F* for fragment and *S* for sentence.

Step 2 Correct each fragment by completing the independent clause or by deleting *who, which,* or *that*. Write the corrected sentences on the lines below.

  _F_   1. Women who work.

  _S_   2. Nowadays, more women work in traditionally male occupations.

  ____   3. For example, the field of medicine.

  ____   4. There are now more women than men in medical school.

  ____   5. Medical schools, which didn't use to accept many women.

  ____   6. Men are also working in traditionally female occupations.

  ____   7. Such as nursing, which used to be a woman's profession.

  ____   8. More women are applying to engineering schools, too.

  ____   9. I know a young woman who is studying construction management.

  ____ 10. Her dream, which is to supervise the construction of bridges and dams.

Corrected sentences:

  1. Women who work have many opportunities these days.

_____

_____

_____

_____

_____

_____

PRACTICE 7

Editing Fragments

Step 1 Read each sentence in the following paragraph. Underline the fragments and write *FRAG* above them. There are five fragments.

Step 2 Then correct each fragment. Write the corrected sentences on the lines below. There is more than one possible way to correct the fragments.

Should Schools Ban Religious Head Coverings?

[1]In my opinion, schools should not ban religious head coverings in school. [2]The most important reason is freedom of religion. [3]Which is guaranteed by the U.S. Constitution. [4]The First Amendment to the Constitution says that people have the right to practice their religion. [5]It says, "Congress shall make no law respecting an establishment of religion,

or prohibiting the free exercise thereof. . . ." ⁶Many religions have special clothing and symbols. ⁷Such as turbans,¹ headscarves, and crosses. ⁸For example, Sikh men must wear turbans to cover their hair. ⁹It is a requirement of their religion. ¹⁰Muslim women may choose to wear scarves on their heads for religious reasons. ¹¹Some Christians, both men and women, like to wear crosses on chains around their necks. ¹²Is their right to follow their beliefs. ¹³Is wrong for a school to take away that right. ¹⁴A second reason is discrimination, which is also against the law. ¹⁵If a school bans only head coverings. ¹⁶This is discrimination. ¹⁷Schools must also ban stars of David, crosses, or any other religious item if they ban head coverings. ¹⁸To sum up, banning religious head coverings is wrong because it violates the law that guarantees freedom of religion and because it discriminates against one group of people.

Corrected sentences:

3. The most important reason is freedom of religion, which is guaranteed by the U.S. Constitution.

¹**turban:** long cloth wrapped around the head; worn by men in some parts of the world

PART 3 | Punctuation

Quotation Marks

In the opinion paragraph that you will write at the end of this chapter, you may want to use quotations from classmates you have interviewed. In this section are the rules for punctuating quotations correctly.

Rules	Examples
1. Put quotation marks before and after another person's exact words.	Classmate Sabrina Reyes says, "Mothers of young children should not work because young children need their mothers at home."
2. Use a "reporting phrase," such as *he says* or *she stated*. The reporting phrase can come before, after, or in the middle of the quotation. Separate it with a comma (or two commas). Another useful reporting phrase is *according to*. If you use someone's exact words after *according to*, use quotation marks.	**She stated,** "It's not easy to be a single mother." "It's not easy," **she stated,** "to be a single mother." "It's not easy to be a single mother," **she stated**. **According to** classmate Sabrina Reyes, "Mothers of young children should not work because young children need their mothers at home."
3. Begin each quotation with a capital letter. When a quoted sentence is separated into two parts, begin the second part with a small letter.	"It's not easy," she stated, "to be a single mother."
4. Commas, periods, and question marks go inside the second quotation mark of a pair.	She said, "Goodbye." "Don't leave so soon," he replied. "Why not**?**" she asked.

PRACTICE 8

Punctuating Quotations

Punctuate the following sentences. Add quotation marks, commas, capital letters, periods, and question marks. One sentence requires a comma but does not require quotation marks or capital letters.

1. Before I came to the United States, my parents said to me, ~~don't~~ "Don't get sick while you are there."

2. Why not I asked

3. Medical care in the United States is too expensive they answered

4. According to a little book about healthcare in the United States a two-hour visit to the emergency room can cost more than $3,000 (*not the exact words*)

5. I asked what happens if I can't pay

6. I don't know my father replied but I think you should find out

7. According to the booklet the school will provide medical insurance while you are a student (*exact words*)

8. My advisor said it doesn't cover everything, so you might want to buy additional insurance from a private company

PART 4 | Writing

Review Questions

Check your understanding of the important points in this chapter by answering the following questions.

Organization

1. What is the difference between a fact and an opinion?
2. Can you use both facts and opinions as support?
3. Which is stronger support?

Sentence Structure

4. Why is an adjective clause called an *adjective* clause?
5. What word introduces adjective clauses that give more information about a person?
6. What two words can introduce an adjective clause that gives more information about a thing?
7. When do you use commas with an adjective clause?
8. Can you use a comma with *that*?
9. What is wrong with the following sentence? *Students who fail the same class three times.* How can you fix it?

Punctuation

10. How do you punctuate a quotation?
11. Give two examples of "reporting phrases."

Writing Assignment

Write a paragraph about a topic from Practice 2 on page 153–155.

Step 1 Prewrite to get ideas.

- You have already written down some ideas. If your teacher allows, interview classmates or take a class survey to get quotations and/or statistics to use as supporting details in your paragraph.
- Organize your ideas into an outline. Make your outline look like the outline on page 151.

Step 2 Write the first draft.

- Write ROUGH DRAFT at the top of your paper.
- Begin your paragraph with a topic sentence that expresses your opinion.
- Add transition signals where they are appropriate.
- Try to include at least two sentences containing adjective clauses.
- Use at least one quotation. Introduce the quotation with a reporting phrase, and use quotation marks.

Step 3 Edit the first draft.

- Edit your paragraph with a partner as you have done in previous chapters. Use the Reader's Response 6B and Writer's Self-Check 6B on pages 212 and 213.

Step 4 Write the final copy.

- Write a neat final copy to hand in to your teacher. Your teacher may also ask you to hand in your prewriting, your outline, and your other drafts.

A Journal Writing[1]

When you learned to speak your first language, you didn't immediately start talking in long, grammatically correct sentences. Instead, you listened and experimented with words and phrases. After a while, you started to speak in sentences, and by the time you started school, you were fluent in the spoken language.

To become fluent in written language, you need to experiment too. Journal writing gives you this opportunity.

How Journal Writing Can Help You

1. You improve your writing by writing. Writing every day will help you become fluent.

2. You choose the topics. In your journal, you can write about topics that are interesting and relevant to your life. You are practicing expressing your ideas and feelings in your journals.

3. Writing a journal can be very enjoyable. You don't have to worry about using a dictionary or checking your grammar or organization and you don't have to write several drafts. You just concentrate on the content.

How to Start

1. Buy an 8½-inch-by-11-inch spiral notebook.

2. Each time you write in your journal, put the date, the time you start, and the time you stop.

3. Don't skip lines.

4. Write for at least an hour a week. You may write for ten minutes each day or for twenty minutes three times a week.

5. Don't worry about making mistakes. Concentrate on your ideas, not on grammar or spelling.

---

[1]This section was adapted from material written by teacher Caroline Gibbs of City College of San Francisco. Used with permission.

6. Try to practice the grammar and new vocabulary or idioms you are learning in class.

7. Write about your daily life, your problems, your feelings, or your opinions. In fact, write about anything that interests you.

8. Your journal will not be shared with other members of the class. Only your teacher will read it.

9. Your teacher will collect your journals regularly, every week or two, to check that you are doing them, to offer advice on your writing, or to respond to your writing. He/she will **not** correct your grammar or spelling although he/she may point out errors that you make repeatedly.

10. If you can't think of a topic to write about, you can choose a topic from the "General Topics" list any time. "Special Topics" are topics that are related to a particular chapter. You could write about one of them after finishing work on that chapter.

General Topics

1. A special skill you have

2. A hobby

3. Why are you studying English? Do you plan to use it in your future job?

4. What is the most difficult part of English for you? Writing? Pronunciation? Vocabulary? Understanding spoken English?

5. Learning to play a sport

6. Your favorite sport to play or watch

7. An accident

8. Being on time

9. The people you live with

10. American customs you like/dislike

11. An important story in the news

12. The working student

13. A big mistake you once made

14. Teenagers

15. The right age to get married

16. A good friend

17. Shopping

18. Your last day in your country

19. Your first day in the United States

20. Discrimination

21. Your favorite food

22. The best car to own

23. A movie star or singer you like

24. A belief that you have or used to have

25. A story from your childhood

26. A favorite possession

27. Music that is special to you

28. A special gift you have given or received

29. A special day or event in your life

30. Your worst habit

31. A frightening experience

32. A funny experience

Special Topics

Chapter 1

Write a "Who Am I?" paragraph about a famous person. Choose a well-known person and give facts about his or her life. Give enough facts so that your teacher and classmates can guess who your person is. Use the sentence-combining exercise you wrote on page 27 as a model.

> I am a famous singer and actress. I am Latin American, and I am from New York. I also design clothes.

Chapter 2

Write about the seasons of the year in your area or in the place where you are from. How many seasons are there? How long does each one last? What is special about each season?

Chapter 3

1. What is your daily routine during the week? Is it the same every day? Does it change on weekends? Write about your activities on a typical weekday and on a typical weekend day. Practice using time clauses and other time expressions.

2. A friend is coming to visit. Plan three days of sightseeing and entertainment for him or her. Practice using capital letters correctly. Include names of places you will visit, restaurants you will eat at, days of the week, street names, and so on.

Chapter 4

1. Write a paragraph describing a favorite picture or photograph. Bring the picture to show to the class and your teacher.

2. Write a short paragraph describing a common object such as a pencil, a wristwatch, or an umbrella. Don't tell what it does. Just describe what it looks like. Don't use the name of the object in your paragraph. In other words, don't use the word *pencil* or *wristwatch*. Instead, use the word "whatsit" (= what is it?). Then read your paragraph to a classmate. Your classmate should be able to guess what you have described.

Example:

A whatsit looks like a long thin stick. It is about 8 inches long, but it can be shorter. It is sometimes round on the outside, but it usually has six sides. It can be any color, but it is often yellow. One end of a whatsit is very pointed and sharp. The other end is soft and rubbery. What is it?

Chapter 5

1. Do you have a love-hate relationship with anything or anyone? Your computer? Your siblings? Write a paragraph about it that is similar to the sentence combining paragraph you wrote on page 138.

2. Write about arranged marriages and marriages "for love." Which do you think is better, and why?

3. A friend has asked you what kind of car to buy. Make a recommendation, and give reasons for your recommendation. Support your reasons with examples.

Chapter 6

Write a letter to Jamila Haddad OR to her parents. Do you think she should go to Lebanon and marry the man, or do you think she should stay in the United States and go to college? Give Jamila OR her parents advice. What should she/they do?

Correction Symbols

Symbol	Meaning	Example of Error	Corrected Sentence
p	punctuation	I live, and go to school here	I live and go to school here.
∧	missing word	am I working in a restaurant.	I am working in a restaurant.
cap	capitalization	cap It is located at main and cap cap cap baker streets in the City.	It is located at Main and Baker Streets in the city.
vt	verb tense	vt I never work as a cashier vt until I get a job there.	I had never worked as a cashier until I got a job there.
s/v agr	subject-verb agreement	s/v agr The manager work hard. s/v agr There is five employees.	The manager works hard. There are five employees.
pron agr	pronoun agreement	Everyone works hard at pron agr their jobs.	All the employees work hard at their jobs.
⌣	connect to make one sentence	We work together. So we have become friends.	We work together, so we have become friends.
sp	spelling	sp The maneger is a woman.	The manager is a woman.
sing/pl	singular or plural	She treats her sing/pl employees like slave.	She treats her employees like slaves.
✕	unnecessary word	My boss she watches everyone all the time.	My boss watches everyone all the time.
wf	wrong word form	wf Her voice is irritated.	Her voice is irritating.

(continued on next page)

Symbol	Meaning	Example of Error	Corrected Sentence
ww	wrong word	The food is delicious. ww <u>Besides</u>, the restaurant is always crowded.	The food is delicious. Therefore, the restaurant is always crowded.
ref	pronoun reference error	The restaurant's specialty is fish. <u>They</u> are always fresh. The food is delicious. Therefore, <u>it</u> is always crowded.	The restaurant's specialty is fish. It is always fresh. The food is delicious. Therefore, the restaurant is always crowded.
wo OR ~	wrong word order	Friday always is our busiest night.	Friday is always our busiest night.
ro	run-on sentence	[Lily was fired she is upset.]	Lily was fired, so she is upset.
cs	comma splice	[Lily was fired, she is upset.]	
frag	fragment	She was fired. [Because she was always late.] [Is open from 6:00 P.M. until the last customer leaves.] [The employees on time and work hard.]	She was fired because she was always late. The restaurant is open from 6:00 P.M. until the last customer leaves. The employees are on time and work hard.
prep	preposition	We start serving dinner 6:00 P.M.	We start serving dinner at 6:00 P.M.
conj	conjunction	Garlic shrimp, fried clams, broiled lobster are the most popular dishes.	Garlic shrimp, fried clams, and broiled lobster are the most popular dishes.

Symbol	Meaning	Example of Error	Corrected Sentence
art	article	Diners in the United States expect glass of water when they first sit down.	Diners in the United States expect a glass of water when they first sit down.
Ⓣ	add a transition	The new employee was careless. She frequently spilled coffee on the table.	The new employee was careless. For example, she frequently spilled coffee on the table.
¶	start a new paragraph		
nfs/nmp	needs further support/needs more proof. You need to add some specific details (examples, facts, quotations) to support your points.		

Grammar Words and Kinds of Sentences

Grammar Words

Adjective	Describes a noun or pronoun	red, hungry, fourth, angry, Canadian *Three little pigs lived in three different houses.*
Adverb	Describes a verb, adjective, or another adverb Tells how, where, or when	beautifully, easily, quickly, very, too, often here, there, everywhere, now, then, later *The ambulance came very quickly.*
Article	Makes a noun specific or general	a, an (general); the (specific) *Please take a piece of fruit from the basket.*
Clause	Contains a subject and a verb	*We sat down. Before we sat down . . .*
Independent clause	Can be a sentence by itself	*We sat down.*
Dependent clause	Begins with a subordinating word; cannot be a sentence by itself	*Before we sat down . . .*
Coordinating conjunction ("Fan boys")	Connects equal elements	for, and, nor, but, or, yet, so *He didn't find them, so he left. Red and blue are my favorite colors.*
Noun	Names a person, place, or thing Is used as a subject or as an object	Alice, book, friendship, fear, education *Alice wrote a book of poems for her friend.*
Preposition	Shows direction, location, ownership, and so on	in, on, at, around, from, by, with, of, because of, next to, according to *He went into his office and looked in every drawer of his desk for the missing contracts.*

Prepositional phrase	Preposition + noun	into his office, of his desk, for a long time
Pronoun	Replaces a noun	he, I, them, it, ours, yours, us, this, that *His secretary had hidden them.*
Subordinating conjunction ("Subordinator")	Is the first word in a dependent clause Makes the clause dependent	when, after, before, as soon as, because, since, if *He didn't find them because his secretary had hidden them.*
Verb	Tells action, feeling, condition OR Links the subject with an adjective	write, is writing, wrote, was writing, can write, has written, is going to write, will write *How many paragraphs have you written? I am going to write a letter tonight.* is, was, has been, seem, appear, feel, look, taste, smell *The baby looks sleepy.*

Kinds of Sentences

In this book, you studied three kinds of sentences in English: simple, compound, and complex.

- A **simple sentence** is one independent clause.

    It's hot today.

    John and Mary are engaged to be married.

    I go to school during the day and work at night.

- A **compound sentence** is two independent clauses joined together by a comma and a coordinating conjunction.

    Her daughter is a doctor, and her son is a dentist.

    Yesterday was a beautiful day, so we went to the beach.

- A **complex sentence** is one independent clause + one (or more) dependent clauses.

    As soon as we arrived, it started to rain.

    The sun came out again after we drove back home.

Conjunctions

Coordinating Conjunctions (Coordinators)

Coordinating conjunctions connect grammatically equal parts of a sentence. The parts can be words, phrases, or clauses. There are seven coordinating conjunctions: *for, and, nor, but, or, yet*, and *so*. We sometimes call them "fan boys" to make it easy to remember them:

for   **a**nd   **n**or   **b**ut   **o**r   **y**et   **s**o

The four coordinating conjunctions covered in this book are *and, but, or*, and *so*.

Coordinating Conjunction	Use	Examples
and	Connects equal similar ideas	John likes to fish **and** hunt. John likes to fish, **and** he often goes fishing.
but	Connects equal different ideas	They were poor **but** happy. The soup was good, **but** it wasn't hot.
or	Connects equal choices	Do you prefer coffee **or** tea? You can renew a driver's license by mail, **or** you can do it in person.
so	Connects a reason to a result	I did not eat breakfast this morning, **so** I am a little hungry.

Subordinating Conjunctions (Subordinators)

A subordinating conjunction is the first word in a dependent clause. Subordinating conjunctions used in this book are the following.

Subordinating Conjunctions	
To tell a time	
after	He goes to school **after** he finishes work.
as soon as	She felt better **as soon as** she took the medicine.
before	**Before** you apply to college, you have to take an entrance exam.
since	It has been a year **since** I left home.
until	We can't leave the room **until** everyone finishes the test.
when	**When** you start college, you usually have to take placement tests in math and English.
whenever	**Whenever** I don't sleep well, I feel sick the next day.
while	Several overcrowded busses passed **while** they were waiting.
To give a reason	
because	Jack excels at sports **because** he trains hard.
since	**Since** she works out daily, Jill is in great condition.
To state a condition	
if	**If** you eat too much sugar, you will gain weight.

Subordinating Words for Adjective Clauses

Adjectives clauses are a kind of dependent clause. The three subordinating words for adjective clauses, which are also called relative pronouns, covered in this book are *who, which*, and *that*.

Relative Pronouns	
To refer to people	
who	Alfredo, **who** is from Switzerland, speaks three languages.
	People **who** speak several languages are valuable employees.
To refer to animals and things	
which that	My new cell phone, **which** I just got yesterday, stopped working today.
	Yesterday I received an e-mail **that** I did not understand.
	Yesterday I received an e-mail **which** I did not understand.

Transition Signals

To show time order	
First, . . .	Next, . . .
First of all, . . .	After that, . . .
Second, . . .	Then . . .
Third, . . .	Finally, . . .

To show listing order	
First, . . .	Also, . . .
First of all, . . .	. . . also . . .
Second, . . .	. . ., also.
Third, . . .	Finally, . . .
In addition, . . .	

To show space order	
On the right, . . .	Above the . . .
On the left, . . .	On one side of the . . .
In the center, . . .	On the other side of the . . .
In the middle, . . .	Opposite the . . .
Next to the . . .	Near the . . .
Beside the . . .	Under the . . .
Between the . . .	

To give a reason
The first reason is (that) . . .
The second reason is (that) . . .
The most important reason is (that) . . .

To give an example	
For example, . . .	. . . such as _____
For instance, . . .	. . ., such as _____
	. . ., for example _____
	. . ., for instance _____

(continued on next page)

To give an opinion	
In my opinion, . . .	I believe (that) . . .
In my view, . . .	I feel (that) . . .
According to _____, . . .	I think (that) . . .
To add a conclusion	
In brief, . . .	To conclude, . . .
Indeed, . . .	To summarize, . . .
In conclusion, . . .	To sum up, . . .
In short, . . .	For these reasons, . . .

Business Letters

A business letter is any letter that is not personal; that is, it is a letter you write to anyone except your family and friends. Business letters in English have a special form.

Study the model and notice the location, spacing, capitalization, and punctuation of the different parts.

MODEL

Business Letter

WRITER'S ADDRESS

DATE

225 Water Street
Boston, MA 12356
December 15, 20____

(SKIP 4 LINES)

RECIPIENT'S ADDRESS

Mr. Daniel Miller
Miller Imports
666 Knoll Lane
Denver, CO 30303

(SKIP 1 LINE)

GREETING

Dear Mr. Miller:

(SKIP 1 LINE)

BEGINNING

I am writing to _____

_____

MIDDLE

_____

_____

_____

_____

(SKIP 1 LINE)

END

Please _____

(SKIP 1 LINE)

LAST SENTENCE

Thank you very much for your time and attention.

(SKIP 1 LINE)

CLOSING

Very truly yours,

HANDWRITTEN SIGNATURE

Robert Henderson

(SKIP 4 LINES)

TYPED NAME

Robert Henderson

(SKIP 1 LINE)

ENCLOSURES

Encl.

Follow these guidelines when you write a business letter.

WRITER'S ADDRESS
DATE

Write or type your address and the date at the top of the page. The number and street are on the first line; the city, state, and zip code are on the second line; and the date is on the third line. Put these three lines at the left side of the page as shown.

RECIPIENT'S ADDRESS

Skip four lines between the date and the name and address of the person you are writing to.

GREETING

Capitalize all of the words in a greeting. Use the last name and title of the person if you know them. Put a colon at the end.

Dear Mr. Smith:

Dear Professor Einstein:

If you don't know the name of the person you are writing to, use a greeting like one of these:

Dear Customer Relations Department:

Dear Miller Imports:

To Whom It May Concern:

BEGINNING

A business letter usually begins with a sentence that directly states the reason you are writing. Do not indent the first sentence. Typical first sentences are like these:

I am writing to complain about . . .

I am writing to request (a refund, information, etc.).

I am writing in response to your ad for a part-time assistant.

MIDDLE

In the middle part of your letter, explain the details of your complaint or request. Be as brief as possible, but give enough details so that the person you are writing to will know what you want him or her to do.

END

At the end of your letter, write exactly what you want the person to do. Start a new paragraph. Do not indent.

Please send the requested information to me at the address shown above.

Please call me at your earliest convenience. My telephone number is . . .

Please send a refund . . .

LAST SENTENCE

End with a polite sentence expressing thanks. A typical ending is

Thank you very much for your time and attention.

CLOSING   Skip one line, and write the closing word or words. Capitalize the first word in the closing and put a comma after it. Standard closings in business letters are these:

> Sincerely,
>
> Sincerely yours,
>
> Very truly yours,
>
> Respectfully,

TYPED NAME
HANDWRITTEN SIGNATURE   Skip four lines and print or type your full name. In the space between the closing and your name, handwrite your name.

ENCLOSURES   If you enclose anything in the envelope with your letter, such as a copy of a disputed bill or your resume, skip one line and write or type the abbreviation *Encl.* below your name.

Reader's Response and Writer's Self-Check Worksheets

Reader's Response 1A
Introducing a Classmate

Reader: _____   **Date:** _____

1. Is the information about you correct?   ☐ **yes**   ☐ **no**

   If your answer is no, what is the correct information?

   _____

   _____

   _____

   _____

   _____

2. Do you understand everything?   ☐ **yes**   ☐ **no**

   If your answer is no, what part(s) or sentence(s) don't you understand?

   _____

   _____

   _____

   _____

   _____

3. What do you like the best about this paragraph? Write one positive comment here:

   _____

   _____

   _____

   _____

Writer: _____   **Date:** _____

Paragraph Form

My paragraph has a title.	☐ yes	☐ no
The title is centered.	☐ yes	☐ no
The first line is indented.	☐ yes	☐ no
There are margins on both sides of the page.	☐ yes	☐ no
The paragraph is double-spaced.	☐ yes	☐ no

Organization

My first sentence gives my classmate's name and tells something about his or her personality.	☐ yes	☐ no
My supporting sentences give information from the interview questions.	☐ yes	☐ no
My concluding sentence tells how I feel about my classmate.	☐ yes	☐ no

Reader's Response 1B
Introducing My Family/a Family Member

Reader: _____   **Date:** _____

1. Does the paragraph give enough information about your classmate's family or family member?   ☐ **yes**   ☐ **no**

   If your answer is no, what else would you like to know?

   _____

   _____

   _____

   _____

   _____

2. Do you understand everything?   ☐ **yes**   ☐ **no**

   If your answer is no, what part(s) or sentence(s) don't you understand?

   _____

   _____

   _____

   _____

   _____

3. What do you like the best about this paragraph? Write one positive comment here:

   _____

   _____

   _____

   _____

Writer: _____   **Date:** _____

Paragraph Form

My paragraph has a title.	☐ yes	☐ no
The title is centered.	☐ yes	☐ no
The first line is indented.	☐ yes	☐ no
There are margins on both sides of the page.	☐ yes	☐ no
The paragraph is double-spaced.	☐ yes	☐ no

Punctuation, Capitalization, and Spelling

I put a period after every sentence.	☐ yes	☐ no
I used capital letters correctly.	☐ yes	☐ no
I checked my spelling.	☐ yes	☐ no

Sentence Structure

Every sentence has at least one SV pair and expresses a complete thought.	☐ yes	☐ no

Grammar

Every student has his or her own personal grammar trouble spots. Some students battle with verb tenses. For others, articles are the main enemy. Some find it hard to know where to put periods.

In the spaces, write down items that you know are problems for you. Then, throughout the term, work on them. Delete items that you have mastered and add new ones that you become aware of.

Personal Grammar Trouble Spots

Number found and corrected

I checked my paragraph for _____ errors.   _____
(verb tense, article, word order, etc.)

I checked my paragraph for _____ errors.   _____

Reader: _____   Date: _____

1. How many main points does the writer make?   **number:** ____

2. Does the writer introduce each main point with a listing-order
   transition signal?   ☐ **yes**   ☐ **no**

   Which signals? Write them here: _____

3. Do you understand everything?   ☐ **yes**   ☐ **no**

   If your answer is no, what part(s) or sentence(s) don't you understand?

   _____

   _____

   _____

   _____

   _____

4. What do you like the best about this paragraph? Write one positive comment here:

   _____

   _____

   _____

   _____

Writer's Self-Check 2A

Title: _____

Writer: _____ **Date:** _____

Paragraph Form

My paragraph looks like the model on page 37. ☐ **yes** ☐ **no**

Organization

My paragraph begins with a topic sentence and ends with a concluding sentence. ☐ **yes** ☐ **no**

My topic sentence has both a topic and a controlling idea. ☐ **yes** ☐ **no**

I use listing order to organize my paragraph. ☐ **yes** ☐ **no**

I use listing-order transition signals to introduce each main point. ☐ **yes** ☐ **no**

Sentence Structure

Every sentence has at least one SV pair and expresses a complete thought. ☐ **yes** ☐ **no**

Punctuation, Capitalization, and Spelling

I put a period after every sentence. ☐ **yes** ☐ **no**

I used capital letters correctly. ☐ **yes** ☐ **no**

I checked my spelling. ☐ **yes** ☐ **no**

Personal Grammar Trouble Spots

Number found and corrected

I checked my paragraph for _____ errors. _____
(verb tense, article, word order, etc.)

I checked my paragraph for _____ errors. _____

Reader's Response 2B

Title: _____

Reader: _____   **Date:** _____

1. How many main points does the writer make?   **number:** ____

2. Does the writer introduce each main point with a listing-order transition signal?   ☐ **yes**   ☐ **no**

   Which signals? Write them here: _____

3. Does each main point have a detail?   ☐ **yes**   ☐ **no**

   Write one detail that you especially like: _____

   _____

4. Do you understand everything?   ☐ **yes**   ☐ **no**

   If your answer is no, what part(s) or sentence(s) don't you understand?

   _____

   _____

   _____

   _____

   _____

5. What do you like the best about this paragraph? Write one positive comment here:

   _____

   _____

   _____

   _____

   _____

Title: _____

Writer: _____   Date: _____

Paragraph Form

My paragraph looks like the model on page 37.   ☐ **yes**   ☐ **no**

Organization

My paragraph begins with a topic sentence and ends with   ☐ **yes**   ☐ **no**
a concluding sentence.

My topic sentence has both a topic and a controlling idea.   ☐ **yes**   ☐ **no**

I use listing order to organize my paragraph.   ☐ **yes**   ☐ **no**

I use listing-order transition signals to introduce each main point.   ☐ **yes**   ☐ **no**

Punctuation, Capitalization, and Spelling

I put a period after every sentence.   ☐ **yes**   ☐ **no**

I used capital letters correctly.   ☐ **yes**   ☐ **no**

I checked my spelling.   ☐ **yes**   ☐ **no**

Sentence Structure

I wrote at least three compound sentences.   ☐ **yes**   ☐ **no**

I checked my paragraph for run-on and comma splice errors.   ☐ **yes**   ☐ **no**

Personal Grammar Trouble Spots

**Number found
and corrected**

I checked my paragraph for _____ errors.   _____
        (verb tense, article, word order, etc.*)*

I checked my paragraph for _____ errors.   _____

Reader: _____   **Date:** _____

1. Does the paragraph begin with a topic sentence?   ☐ **yes**   ☐ **no**

    Copy the topic sentence here: _____

    _____

2. Do you understand everything?   ☐ **yes**   ☐ **no**

    If your answer is no, what part(s) or sentence(s) don't you understand?

    _____

    _____

    _____

    _____

    _____

3. Does the paragraph have time-order signals or listing-order signals?

                                                    ☐ **time order**   ☐ **listing order**

    Write three of the transition signals here:

    _____

4. What do you like the best about this paragraph? Write one positive comment here:

    _____

    _____

    _____

    _____

    _____

Writer: _____   **Date:** _____

Paragraph Form

My paragraph looks like the model on page 68.   ☐ yes   ☐ no

Organization

My paragraph begins with a "how to" topic sentence.   ☐ yes   ☐ no

The steps are in either time order or listing order.   ☐ yes   ☐ no

I used transition signals with some of the steps.   ☐ yes   ☐ no

I wrote a concluding sentence.   ☐ yes   ☐ no

Sentence Structure

Every sentence has at least one SV pair and expresses
a complete thought.   ☐ yes   ☐ no

Punctuation, Capitalization, and Spelling

I put a period after every sentence.   ☐ yes   ☐ no

I used capital letters correctly.   ☐ yes   ☐ no

I checked my spelling.   ☐ yes   ☐ no

Personal Grammar Trouble Spots

**Number found
and corrected**

I checked my paragraph for _____ errors.   _____
    (verb tense, article, word order, etc.)

I checked my paragraph for _____ errors.   _____

How to _____

Reader: _____   **Date:** _____

1. What is the topic of this paragraph?   How to _____

2. Does the paragraph begin with a topic sentence?   ☐ **yes**   ☐ **no**

   Copy the topic sentence here: _____

   _____

3. Do you understand everything?   ☐ **yes**   ☐ **no**

   If your answer is no, what part(s) or sentence(s) don't you understand?

   _____

   _____

   _____

   _____

4. Does the paragraph have transition signals (*first, next, then*, and so on)
   to help you understand each step?   ☐ **yes**   ☐ **no**

5. What do you like the best about this paragraph? Write one positive comment here:

   _____

   _____

   _____

   _____

   _____

Writer: _____ **Date:** _____

Paragraph Form

My paragraph looks like the model on page 68. ☐ **yes** ☐ **no**

Organization

My paragraph begins with a "how to" topic sentence. ☐ **yes** ☐ **no**

The steps are in time order. ☐ **yes** ☐ **no**

I used time-order signals with some of the steps. ☐ **yes** ☐ **no**

Sentence Structure

Every sentence has at least one SV pair and expresses a complete thought. ☐ **yes** ☐ **no**

I wrote at least three complex sentences, and I punctuated them correctly. ☐ **yes** ☐ **no**

I checked my paragraph for sentence errors: run-ons, comma splices, and fragments. ☐ **yes** ☐ **no**

Punctuation, Capitalization, and Spelling

I put a period after every sentence. ☐ **yes** ☐ **no**

I used capital letters correctly. ☐ **yes** ☐ **no**

I checked my spelling. ☐ **yes** ☐ **no**

Personal Grammar Trouble Spots

Number found and corrected

I checked my paragraph for _____ errors. _____
(verb tense, article, word order, etc.)

I checked my paragraph for _____ errors. _____

Reader: _____   **Date:** _____

1. What room does the writer describe? _____

2. Does the paragraph begin with a topic sentence?   ☐ **yes**   ☐ **no**

   Copy the topic sentence here: _____

   _____

3. Do you understand everything?   ☐ **yes**   ☐ **no**

   If your answer is no, what part(s) or sentence(s) don't you understand?

   _____

   _____

   _____

   _____

4. Does the writer use space order?   ☐ **yes**   ☐ **no**
   Write three space-order signals that you remember:

   _____

5. What adjectives does the writer use in his or her description? Write three adjectives that you remember:

   _____

6. What do you like the best about this paragraph? Write one positive comment here:

   _____

   _____

   _____

   _____

   _____

Writer: _____   **Date:** _____

Paragraph Form

My paragraph looks like the model on page 99.   ☐ yes   ☐ no

Organization

My paragraph begins with a topic sentence and ends with
a concluding sentence.   ☐ yes   ☐ no

I use space order to organize my description.   ☐ yes   ☐ no

I used lots of details to make my reader "see" the room.   ☐ yes   ☐ no

Grammar

I used adjectives to describe different objects in the room.   ☐ yes   ☐ no

I was careful to put cumulative adjectives in the correct order
and to put commas between coordinate adjectives.   ☐ yes   ☐ no

Sentence Structure

Every sentence has at least one SV pair and expresses
a complete thought.   ☐ yes   ☐ no

I wrote different kinds of sentences—simple, compound,
and complex.   ☐ yes   ☐ no

I checked my paragraph for sentence errors: run-ons,
comma splices, and fragments.   ☐ yes   ☐ no

Punctuation, Capitalization, and Spelling

I put a period after every sentence.   ☐ yes   ☐ no

I used capital letters correctly.   ☐ yes   ☐ no

I checked my spelling.   ☐ yes   ☐ no

Personal Grammar Trouble Spots

**Number found
and corrected**

I checked my paragraph for _____ errors.   _____
            (verb tense, article, word order, etc.)

I checked my paragraph for _____ errors.   _____

Reader: _____   **Date:** _____

1. What place does the writer describe? _____

2. Does the paragraph begin with a topic sentence? ☐ **yes**   ☐ **no**

   Copy the topic sentence here: _____
   _____

3. Do you understand everything? ☐ **yes**   ☐ **no**

   If your answer is no, what part(s) or sentence(s) don't you understand?

   _____
   _____
   _____
   _____
   _____

4. Does the writer use space order? ☐ **yes**   ☐ **no**

   Write three space-order signals that you remember:

   _____

5. What adjectives does the writer use in his or her description? Write three adjectives that you remember:

   _____

6. What do you like the best about this paragraph? Write one positive comment here:

   _____
   _____
   _____
   _____
   _____

Writer's Self-Check 4B

Title: _____

Writer: _____   **Date:** _____

Paragraph Form

My paragraph looks like the model on page 99.   ☐ yes   ☐ no

Organization

My paragraph begins with a topic sentence and ends with a concluding sentence.   ☐ yes   ☐ no

I use space order to organize my description.   ☐ yes   ☐ no

I used lots of details to make my reader "see" the room.   ☐ yes   ☐ no

Grammar

I used adjectives to describe different objects in the room.   ☐ yes   ☐ no

I was careful to put cumulative adjectives in the correct order and to put commas between coordinate adjectives.   ☐ yes   ☐ no

Sentence Structure

Every sentence has at least one SV pair and expresses a complete thought.   ☐ yes   ☐ no

I wrote different kinds of sentences—simple, compound, and complex.   ☐ yes   ☐ no

I began some sentences with a prepositional phrase.   ☐ yes   ☐ no

I checked my paragraph for sentence errors: run-ons, comma splices, and fragments.   ☐ yes   ☐ no

Punctuation, Capitalization, and Spelling

I put a period after every sentence.   ☐ yes   ☐ no

I used capital letters correctly.   ☐ yes   ☐ no

I checked my spelling.   ☐ yes   ☐ no

Personal Grammar Trouble Spots

Number found and corrected

I checked my paragraph for _____ errors.   _____
(verb tense, article, word order, etc.)

I checked my paragraph for _____ errors.   _____

Reader: _____   **Date:** _____

1. How many reasons does the writer give?   **number:** ____

2. Does the writer introduce each reason with a transition signal?   ☐ **yes**   ☐ **no**

    Which signals? Write them here: _____

3. Does each reason have an example?   ☐ **yes**   ☐ **no**

    Write one example that you especially like: _____

    _____

4. Do you understand everything?   ☐ **yes**   ☐ **no**

    If your answer is no, what part(s) or sentence(s) don't you understand?

    _____

    _____

    _____

    _____

    _____

5. What do you like the best about this paragraph? Write one positive comment here:

    _____

    _____

    _____

    _____

    _____

Writer: _____   **Date:** _____

Paragraph Form

My paragraph looks like the model on page 124.   ☐ yes   ☐ no

Organization

My paragraph begins with a topic sentence and ends with a concluding sentence.   ☐ yes   ☐ no

I used listing order to organize the reasons.   ☐ yes   ☐ no

I used transition signals to introduce each reason.   ☐ yes   ☐ no

I used at least one example or other specific detail for each reason.   ☐ yes   ☐ no

Sentence Structure

Every sentence has at least one SV pair and expresses a complete thought.   ☐ yes   ☐ no

I wrote different kinds of sentences—simple, compound, and complex.   ☐ yes   ☐ no

I checked my paragraph for sentence errors: run-ons, comma splices, and fragments.   ☐ yes   ☐ no

Punctuation, Capitalization, and Spelling

I put a period after every sentence.   ☐ yes   ☐ no

I used capital letters correctly.   ☐ yes   ☐ no

I checked my spelling.   ☐ yes   ☐ no

Personal Grammar Trouble Spots

Number found and corrected

I checked my paragraph for _____ errors.   _____
(verb tense, article, word order, etc.)

I checked my paragraph for _____ errors.   _____

Reader: _____   **Date:** _____

1. How many reasons does the writer give?   **number:** _____

2. Does the writer introduce each reason with a transition signal?   ☐ **yes**   ☐ **no**

   Which signals? Write them here: _____

3. Does each reason have an example?   ☐ **yes**   ☐ **no**

   Write one example that you especially like: _____

   _____

4. Do you understand everything?   ☐ **yes**   ☐ **no**

   If your answer is no, what part(s) or sentence(s) don't you understand?

   _____

   _____

   _____

   _____

   _____

5. What do you like the best about this paragraph? Write one positive comment here:

   _____

   _____

   _____

   _____

   _____

Writer's Self-Check 5B

Title: _____

Writer: _____   **Date:** _____

Paragraph Form

My paragraph looks like the model on page 124.   ☐ yes   ☐ no

Organization

My paragraph begins with a topic sentence and ends with a concluding sentence.   ☐ yes   ☐ no

I used listing order to organize the reasons.   ☐ yes   ☐ no

I used transition signals to introduce each reason.   ☐ yes   ☐ no

I used at least one example or other specific detail for each reason.   ☐ yes   ☐ no

Punctuation, Capitalization, and Spelling

I checked my paragraph for correct punctuation, capitalization, and spelling.   ☐ yes   ☐ no

Sentence Structure

Every sentence has at least one SV pair and expresses a complete thought.   ☐ yes   ☐ no

I wrote different kinds of sentences—simple, compound, and complex.   ☐ yes   ☐ no

I checked my paragraph for sentence errors: run-ons, comma splices, and fragments.   ☐ yes   ☐ no

Personal Grammar Trouble Spots

Number found and corrected

I checked my paragraph for _____ errors.   _____
(verb tense, article, word order, etc.)

I checked my paragraph for _____ errors.   _____

Reader: _____ **Date:** _____

1. How many reasons does the writer give? **number:** _____

2. Does the writer introduce each reason with a transition signal? ☐ **yes** ☐ **no**

   Which signals? Write them here: _____

3. Does each reason have support? ☐ **yes** ☐ **no**

   Write one example that you especially like: _____

   _____

4. Do you understand everything? ☐ **yes** ☐ **no**

   If your answer is no, what part(s) or sentence(s) don't you understand?

   _____

   _____

   _____

   _____

   _____

5. What do you like the best about this paragraph? Write one positive comment here:

   _____

   _____

   _____

   _____

Writer's Self-Check 6A

Title: _____

Writer: _____ **Date:** _____

Paragraph Form

My paragraph looks like the model on page 150.   ☐ yes   ☐ no

Organization

My paragraph begins with a topic sentence and ends with a concluding sentence.   ☐ yes   ☐ no

I used listing order to organize the reasons.   ☐ yes   ☐ no

I used transition signals to introduce each reason.   ☐ yes   ☐ no

I used one or two supporting details for each reason.   ☐ yes   ☐ no

Punctuation, Capitalization, and Spelling

I checked my paragraph for correct punctuation, capitalization, and spelling.   ☐ yes   ☐ no

Sentence Structure

Every sentence has at least one SV pair and expresses a complete thought.   ☐ yes   ☐ no

I wrote different kinds of sentences—simple, compound, and complex.   ☐ yes   ☐ no

I checked my paragraph for sentence errors: fragments, run-ons, and comma splices.   ☐ yes   ☐ yes

Personal Grammar Trouble Spots

Number found and corrected

I checked my paragraph for _____ errors.   _____
   (*verb tense, article, word order*, etc.)

I checked my paragraph for _____ errors.   _____

Reader: _____ **Date:** _____

1. How many reasons does the writer give?   **number:** ____

2. Does the writer introduce each reason with a transition signal?   ☐ **yes**   ☐ **no**

   Which signals? Write them here: _____

3. Does each reason have supporting facts?   ☐ **yes**   ☐ **no**

   Does the writer use at least one quotation?   ☐ **yes**   ☐ **no**

4. Do you understand everything?   ☐ **yes**   ☐ **no**

   If your answer is no, what part(s) or sentence(s) don't you understand?

   _____

   _____

   _____

   _____

   _____

5. What do you like the best about this paragraph? Write one positive comment here:

   _____

   _____

   _____

   _____

   _____

Writer's Self-Check 6B

Title: _____

Writer: _____   Date: _____

Paragraph Form

My paragraph looks like the model on page 150.   ☐ **yes**   ☐ **no**

Organization

My paragraph begins with a clear opinion topic sentence.   ☐ **yes**   ☐ **no**

I used transition signals to introduce each reason.   ☐ **yes**   ☐ **no**

I used one or two supporting details for each reason.   ☐ **yes**   ☐ **no**

I used at least one quotation.   ☐ **yes**   ☐ **no**

Punctuation, Capitalization, and Spelling

I checked my paragraph for correct punctuation, capitalization, and spelling.   ☐ **yes**   ☐ **no**

Sentence Structure

I wrote different kinds of sentences—simple, compound, and complex.   ☐ **yes**   ☐ **no**

I wrote at least two sentences containing adjective clauses.   ☐ **yes**   ☐ **no**

I checked my paragraph for sentence errors: fragments, run-ons, and comma splices.   ☐ **yes**   ☐ **no**

Personal Grammar Trouble Spots

Number found and corrected

I checked my paragraph for _____ errors.   _____
(verb tense, article, word order, etc.)

I checked my paragraph for _____ errors.   _____

Index

Notes

Notes

Notes

Notes

Notes